Steck-Vaughn

Language

Exercises

Book 3

Harcourt Achieve

Rigby • Saxon • Steck-Vaughn

www.HarcourtAchieve.com
1.800.531.5015

Acknowledgments

Illustrations: Eric Zill

Photography: P. 5 Phyllis Liedeker; p. 6 Rick Williams; p. 8 Rick Williams; p. 19 American History Museum, Smithsonian Institution; p. 21 Bob Daemmrich; p. 31 NASA; p. 34 © John Chellman/Animals Animals; p. 36 Carlos Vergara; p. 37 © Joe McDonald/Animals Animals; p. 39 Cooke Photographic; p. 40 Texas Highway Department; p. 47 Michael Patrick; p. 51 Sandy Wilson; p. 59 © Max Gibbs/Animals Animals.

Additional photography by BrandX/Getty Royalty Free; Digital Vision/Getty Royalty Free; Photodisc/Getty Royalty Free.

Macmillan/McGraw-Hill School Publishing Company: Pronunciation Key, reprinted with permission of the publisher, from *Macmillan School Dictionary 1.* Copyright © 1990 Macmillan Publishing Company, a division of Macmillan, Inc.

LANGUAGE EXERCISES Series:

Book 1	Book 4	Book 7
Book 2	Book 5	Book 8
Book 3	Book 6	Review

ISBN 978-1-4190-1871-8
ISBN 1-4190-1871-X

7 8 0982 12 11
4500295074

Table of Contents

Check What You Know........................ 1
Check What You Know
  Correlation Chart......................... 4

Unit 1 Vocabulary

1 ▪ Synonyms................................. 5
2 ▪ Antonyms 6
3 ▪ Homonyms 7
4 ▪ More Homonyms 8
5 ▪ Words with More Than One
  Meaning 9
6 ▪ Prefixes 10
7 ▪ Suffixes 11
8 ▪ Compound Words 12
9 ▪ Contractions 13
Review 14
Using What You've Learned 16

Unit 2 Sentences

10 ▪ Sentences 18
11 ▪ Identifying Sentences 19
12 ▪ Statements and Questions 20
13 ▪ Commands and Exclamations.........21
14 ▪ Subjects in Sentences 22
15 ▪ Predicates in Sentences 23
16 ▪ Combining Subjects and Predicates ...24
17 ▪ Combining Sentences 25
18 ▪ Writing Clear Sentences...............26
Review.......................................27
Using What You've Learned 29

Unit 3 Grammar and Usage

19 ▪ Nouns...................................31
20 ▪ Singular and Plural Nouns 32

21 ▪ Common and Proper Nouns 33
22 ▪ Action Verbs............................34
23 ▪ Verbs in the Present...................35
24 ▪ Verbs in the Past.......................36
25 ▪ Linking Verbs...........................37
26 ▪ Using Am, Is, and Are.................38
27 ▪ Using Was and Were 39
28 ▪ Helping Verbs..........................40
29 ▪ Using Forms of Do and See...........41
30 ▪ Using Forms of Give and Go..........42
31 ▪ Pronouns...............................43
32 ▪ Subject and Object Pronouns 44
33 ▪ Possessive Pronouns...................45
34 ▪ Using I or Me...........................46
35 ▪ Adjectives...............................47
36 ▪ Comparing with Adjectives............48
37 ▪ Using A or An...........................49
38 ▪ Adverbs.................................50
39 ▪ Using Good and Well...................51
Review 52
Using What You've Learned..................54

Unit 4 Capitalization and Punctuation

40 ▪ Capitalizing Days, Holidays,
  and Months 56
41 ▪ Capitalizing Names of People
  and Places 57
42 ▪ Beginning Sentences 58
43 ▪ Ending Sentences 59
44 ▪ Abbreviating Names of People and
  Places 60
45 ▪ Abbreviating Names of Days
  and Months 61
46 ▪ Using Commas in Sentences...........62
47 ▪ Writing Letters Correctly...............63
48 ▪ Using Apostrophes to Show
  Ownership..............................64
49 ▪ Using Apostrophes in Contractions.....65
50 ▪ Using Quotation Marks.................66
Review 67
Using What You've Learned.................69

Unit 5 Composition

51 ▪ Writing Sentences 71
52 ▪ Writing Paragraphs 72
53 ▪ Writing Topic Sentences 73
54 ▪ Writing Details 74
55 ▪ Arranging Details in Order 75
56 ▪ Writing with Purpose 76
57 ▪ Choosing a Topic 77
58 ▪ How-to Paragraph 78
59 ▪ Writing a How-to Paragraph 79
60 ▪ Writing an Invitation 80
61 ▪ Writing a Telephone Message 81
Review 82
Using What You've Learned 84

Unit 6 Study Skills

62 ▪ Following Directions 86
63 ▪ Following Written Directions 87
64 ▪ Grouping 88
65 ▪ Using a Table of Contents 89
66 ▪ Using an Index 90
67 ▪ Alphabetical Order 91
68 ▪ Guide Words 92
69 ▪ Dictionary: Definitions 93
70 ▪ Dictionary: Pronunciation 95
Review 96
Using What You've Learned 98

Final Reviews

Unit 1 100
Unit 2 102
Unit 3 104
Unit 4 106
Unit 5 108
Unit 6 110

Check What You've Learned 112
Check What You've Learned
    Correlation Chart 115

Answer Key 116

Index ....Inside Back Cover

A. Write S before each pair of synonyms, A before each pair of antonyms, and H before each pair of homonyms.

_____ **1.** up, down   _____ **3.** light, dark

_____ **2.** tale, tail   _____ **4.** yell, shout

B. Read the meanings. Write the number of the meaning of each underlined word.

_____ **1.** Tim drew <u>straight</u> lines.

_____ **2.** I tried to get a <u>straight</u> answer.

> **straight 1.** a line without curves. **2.** to go directly to a place. **3.** in an honest way.

C. Write P before each word with a prefix, S before each word with a suffix, and C before each compound word.

_____ **1.** underground   _____ **3.** unable

_____ **2.** pitcher   _____ **4.** review

D. Write the words that make up each contraction.

1. isn't _____ _____   **3.** you're _____ _____

2. I'll _____ _____   **4.** that's _____ _____

E. Write S before the statement, Q before the question, C before the command, and E before the exclamation. Then underline the subject, and circle the predicate in each sentence.

_____ **1.** That is an amazing sight!

_____ **2.** What do you think that thing is?

_____ **3.** It looks like some kind of spaceship.

_____ **4.** Protect your eyes from the bright lights.

F. Combine the sentences. Write the new sentence.

1. The weather is hot. The weather is humid.

_____

2. The sun might shine. It might rain.

_____

G. Read the sentences. Write two sentences for each.

1. Osato has a vegetable garden, she waters it every day.

_____

_____

2. Gary bakes bread, he uses it when he makes sandwiches.

_____

_____

H. Write S before each singular noun and P before each plural noun. Then circle the common nouns, and underline the proper nouns.

_____ 1. taxes   _____ 3. computer

_____ 2. Eduardo   _____ 4. Andes Mountains

I. Write A if the underlined verb is an action verb, L if it is a linking verb, or H if it is a helping verb.

_____ 1. The plants grew by the stream.

_____ 2. The animals were by the stream.

_____ 3. They are eating the plants.

J. Write past or present on the lines.

_____ 1. Martin jogs at least two miles every day.

_____ 2. Last week he jogged a total of 15 miles.

K. Circle the correct pronoun in each sentence.

1. Mr. Kelso and (I, me) are neighbors.
2. (Him, He) is a very kind man.
3. I always enjoy talking to (his, him).

L. On the line before each sentence, write <u>adjective</u> or <u>adverb</u> to describe the underlined word.

_____ 1. This box is <u>heavier</u> than the other one.

_____ 2. The worker <u>carefully</u> picked up the box.

M. In the letter below, underline the letters that should be capitalized, and add punctuation where needed.

1748 e first st
kansas city missouri 64114
jan 12 2006

dear mr haas

thank you for setting up an interview with me for next

tuesday_____ yes ive done well here working on

televisions radios and dvd players_____ did you

know that im learning how to work on computers_____ it is

easier than i thought_____ i fixed my friends computer last

week_____ ill tell you more about this on tuesday_____

sincerely

william thurston

N. Write a topic sentence and a sentence with supporting details on the topic of crime.

_____

_____

O. Number the following directions in order.

_____ 1. Then sign the bottom of the form.

_____ 2. Finally, turn the form in at the downtown office.

_____ 3. First, fill out the application form.

P. Write the words in alphabetical order.

1. money _____

2. manage _____

3. mention _____

4. mystery _____

Q. Use the dictionary entries to answer the questions.

1. Which word has one definition? _____

2. Which word has three definitions? _____

3. Which word means "a small building?"_____

> **sharp 1.** having a point or edge that can cut. **2.** to turn in a sudden way. **3.** to be somewhere at an exact time.
> **shave** to cut hair with a razor
> **shed 1.** to lose or drop off **2.** a small building

Below is a list of the sections on *Check What You Know* and the pages on which the skills in each section are taught. If you missed any questions, turn to the pages listed, and practice the skills. Then correct the problems you missed on *Check What You Know*.

Section	Practice Page	Section	Practice Page	Section	Practice Page
Unit 1		F	24–25	*Unit 4*	
A	5–8	G	26	M	56–66
B	9	*Unit 3*		*Unit 5*	
C	10–12	H	31–33	N	72–75
D	13	I	34–42	*Unit 6*	
		J	35, 36	O	75, 86, 87
Unit 2		K	43–46	P	91
E	20–23	L	47–51	Q	93, 94

> - A **synonym** is a word that means the same or almost the same thing as another word.
>   EXAMPLES: small—little   jump—leap

- **Write synonyms for the words shown under the lines. Choose the synonyms from the box.**

beneath	odd	tiny	done
large	started	supper	repair

I sat down to eat my _____. Suddenly, I heard

dinner

an _____ noise. The noise came from

unusual

_____ the kitchen sink. I was worried that I had

under

a _____ crack in the pipe. But I saw that it was

huge

just a _____ leak. I _____ to work

little   began

on the leak. It did not take long to _____ the

fix

pipe. I was _____ in just a few minutes.

finished

- **Write a sentence using the synonyms <u>great</u> and <u>wonderful</u>. Tell about something you like to do.**

_____

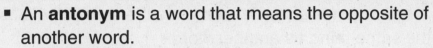
- An **antonym** is a word that means the opposite of another word.
  - EXAMPLES: on–off   wet–dry

- **Write antonyms for the words shown under the lines. Choose the antonyms from the box.**

bottom	buy	easy	subtract	give

It is _____ to use a checkbook. I write
       hard

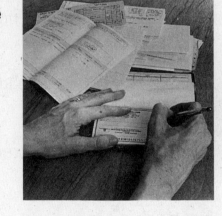

checks for the things I _____ . I make sure
        sell

I sign my name at the _____ of the check.
        top

I _____ the check to the store clerk. Then
  take

I _____ the amount of the check from my
  add

balance.

- **Write the sentences. Complete each one with an antonym for the underlined word.**

1. Do you think Ann will <u>win</u> or (lose, leave)?

_____

2. Will he <u>return</u> to work <u>now</u> or (today, later)?

_____

Homonyms

> ■ A **homonym** is a word that sounds the same as another word but has a different spelling and a different meaning.
>
> EXAMPLES: **they're, their, there**
> Use they're to mean "they are."
> **They're** playing now.
> Use their to mean "belonging to them."
> Did they bring **their** bats?
> Use there to mean "in that place" or to help begin a thought.
> He threw it **there**. **There** are two teams.

■ **Write they're, their, or there.**

1. Lee and Vin walk down the street carrying

   _____ baseball gloves.

2. "All the players are _____

   in the park," said Lee.

3. "I hope _____ ready for the big game today," replied Vin.

4. All the players quickly took _____ places on the field.

5. "Look, _____ are people cheering for us!" cried Vin.

6. "I think _____ here to see us win the game," said Lee.

7. Vin and Lee's team won _____ game by one run.

■ **Write a sentence about a baseball game using they're, their, or there.**

_____

> - Remember that a homonym is a word that sounds the same as another word.
>
>   EXAMPLES: **hear, here   to, two, too**
>   Use <u>hear</u> to mean "to listen to."
>   Did you **hear** that funny song?
>   Use <u>here</u> to mean "in this place."
>   The tapes are over **here**.
>
>   Use <u>to</u> to mean "toward" or to go with words like <u>make</u> and <u>buy</u>.
>   Juan rode his bike **to** the store. He wanted **to** buy a CD.
>   Use <u>too</u> to mean "more than enough" or "also."
>   The music is **too** loud. I like that song, **too**.
>   Use <u>two</u> to mean "the number 2."
>   Those **two** speakers sound very good.

- **Underline the correct homonym in each sentence.**

1. Lisa and Kamal were driving (too, to, two) the bank.

2. They were listening (to, two, too) some music.

3. Kamal said, "I (here, hear) a song I like."

4. Lisa said she liked that song, (two, to, too).

5. They decided (to, too, two) go to a music store.

6. In just (too, to, two) minutes, they were at the store.

7. They looked (their, there) for a parking space.

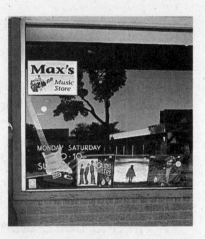

8. Lisa made (to, two, too) right turns as they looked.

9. Then she found a space, but it was (too, to, two) small.

10. Kamal pointed (two, too, to) a larger space.

11. It would be easier to park (hear, here).

12. Now they were ready (two, too, to) buy a compact disc.

Lesson 5

Words with More Than One Meaning

- Many words have more than one meaning.
  EXAMPLE: Pound means "a weight that is equal to 16 ounces." Buy a **pound** of peanuts. Pound also means "to hit hard over and over." **Pound** the stake into the ground.

- **Read the meanings on the right. Write the number of the meaning for each underlined word.**

1. Anna showed her son how to spin a top. _____

2. They heard their dog bark. _____

3. Anna turned on the outside light. _____

4. She saw that a strong wind had knocked over the light doghouse. _____

5. The dog watched a squirrel climb up the bark of the tree. _____

6. The squirrel climbed to the top of the tree. _____

7. The squirrel was light enough to jump onto a thin branch. _____

8. But there wasn't enough light to see where the squirrel went next. _____

light
1. not heavy
2. something by which we see

bark
1. hard outside covering of a tree
2. the sound a dog makes

top
1. the highest part
2. a toy

- **Write a sentence using the first meaning of light.**

_____

> ■ A **prefix** is a word part added to the beginning of a base word to change the meaning of the word.
>
> EXAMPLES: The prefix un- means "not" or "the opposite of." The prefix re- means "again."
>
> un- + usual = **un**usual, meaning "not usual"
>
> re- + heat = **re**heat, meaning "heat again"

■ **Add the prefix un- to the words below. Then write the meaning of the new word.**

1. happy _____

2. fair _____

3. even _____

4. safe _____

5. fit _____

■ **Add the prefix re- to the words below. Then write the meaning of the new word.**

1. open _____

2. test _____

3. use _____

4. read _____

■ **Write one sentence with a word that has the prefix un-. Write one sentence with a word that has the prefix re-.**

1. _____

2. _____

- A **suffix** is a word part added to the end of a base word to change the meaning of the word.

    EXAMPLES: The suffixes -er and -or mean "a person or thing that _____ ."

    heat + er = heat**er**, meaning "a thing that heats"

    sail + or = sail**or**, meaning "a person that sails"

- **Add the suffixes to the words to make new words.**

1. climb + er = _____   5. act + or = _____

2. teach + er = _____   6. mark + er = _____

3. visit + or = _____   7. paint + er = _____

4. travel + er = _____   8. sing + er = _____

- **Write each sentence with a new word made by adding -er to the word in ( ).**

1. The _____ clipped the roses.   (garden)

_____

2. He cleaned his gloves in the _____.   (wash)

_____

3. He and a _____ ate lunch.   (farm)

_____

4. Then he hired a new _____ to help him.   (work)

_____

5. His new helper used to be a _____.   (teach)

Compound Words

> - A **compound word** is made by joining one word with another word.
>   EXAMPLES: air + plane = airplane
>   sun + set = sunset

- **Write the compound word made by joining each pair of words.**

1. birth + day = _____

2. after + noon = _____

3. farm + house = _____

4. fire + place = _____

5. cat + fish = _____

6. rain + bow = _____

7. thunder + storm = _____

8. sun + rise = _____

9. water + fall = _____

10. down + stairs = _____

- **Underline the compound word in each sentence. Then write the two words that form the compound word.**

1. The birthday party is a surprise. _____ _____

2. Is everyone here? _____ _____

3. Let's hide inside the house! _____ _____

4. Everything is ready. _____ _____

5. The doorbell rings. _____ _____

6. Nobody leaves their hiding place. _____ _____

7. Somebody needs to open the door! _____ _____

> - A **contraction** is a word made by joining two words. When the words are joined, one or more letters are left out. An **apostrophe** (') shows where the missing letter or letters would be.
>
>   EXAMPLES: I + will = I'll, there + is = there's, is + not = isn't

- **Rewrite the sentences. Use contractions in place of the underlined words.**

doesn't	Here's	I'll	isn't	she'll	She's	There's

1. <u>She is</u> going camping this weekend.

   _____

2. I think <u>she will</u> go fishing in the lake.

   _____

3. Inuk <u>does not</u> like to fish.

   _____

4. <u>Here is</u> some fresh bait.

   _____

5. <u>There is</u> enough for everyone to use.

   _____

6. After we catch the fish, <u>I will</u> help cook them.

   _____

7. It <u>is not</u> hard to do.

   _____

- **Write a sentence telling what you will do this weekend. Use the contraction I'll.**

   _____

■ **Write the synonym for each underlined word.**

1. I have nothing to eat in my <u>house</u>.   (home, store) _____

2. I will go to the <u>store</u> to buy some food.   (market, garden) _____

3. I need a <u>bag</u> of potatoes.   (box, sack) _____

4. I like the <u>large</u> grapefruit best.   (big, small) _____

5. These melons look <u>good</u>.   (nice, sour) _____

■ **Write the antonym for each underlined word.**

1. What time does the store <u>close</u>?   (shut, open) _____

2. I don't want to be <u>late</u>.   (slow, early) _____

3. It is such a <u>sunny</u> day.   (clear, rainy) _____

4. I think I will <u>walk</u> to the store.   (run, stroll) _____

5. I don't have far to <u>go</u>.   (start, stop) _____

■ **Choose and underline the correct word in each sentence.**

1. I see (to, two, too) friends at the store.

2. I didn't know they would be (hear, here).

3. They need to buy some food, (too, to, two).

4. We walk over (two, too, to) the frozen foods.

5. We stop (their, there, they're) to visit.

6. Now my friends are done, and (they're, their, there) ready to leave.

7. I am ready to leave, (to, two, too).

- **Write two sentences. Use a different meaning for <u>pound</u> in each sentence.**

  1. _____

  2. _____

- **Write two sentences. Use a different meaning for <u>match</u> in each sentence.**

  1. _____

  2. _____

- **Underline each word that begins with a prefix.**

1. pack, unpack	4. relive, live	7. rename, name
2. copy, recopy	5. make, remake	8. true, untrue
3. untie, tie	6. take, retake	9. unsure, sure

- **Underline each word that ends with a suffix.**

1. clean, cleaner	4. teacher, teach	7. heater, heat
2. visitor, visit	5. dry, dryer	8. lead, leader
3. work, worker	6. act, actor	9. sailor, sail

- **Underline each contraction. Circle each compound word.**

1. I'd like a weekend job.	4. There's a job with the railroad.
2. Isn't there one in the newspaper?	5. I can't go today.
3. Yes, here's something.	6. I'll go Monday afternoon.

- **Rewrite the letter. Use a homonym for the words in dark print. Use a contraction for the words that are underlined.**

> Dear Mr. Jones,
>   Please tell your workers **their** making **two** much noise. I **here** them early in the morning. **There** always waking me up, and I <u>cannot</u> go back to sleep. I <u>should not</u> have to listen to **they're** noise. I <u>do not</u> think they should start working **hear** until 8 o'clock. I <u>am</u> sure we can find a way **too** solve this problem.

_____

_____

_____

_____

_____

_____

_____

_____

_____

_____

■ Write a paragraph about your favorite meal.
Include these words in your paragraph:

1. a synonym of <u>large</u>   **4.** a compound word

2. an antonym of <u>cold</u>   **5.** a word with the prefix <u>re</u>- or <u>un</u>-

3. the homonyms <u>to</u>, <u>too</u>, and <u>two</u>   **6.** a word with the suffix -<u>er</u> or -<u>or</u>

_____

_____

_____

_____

_____

_____

_____

_____

_____

_____

_____

_____

_____

_____

_____

_____

> ▪ A **sentence** is a group of words that tells or asks
> something. It stands for a complete thought.
>   EXAMPLE: Rosa dreamed about the picnic.

▪ **Underline the sentences.**

1. Daniel and Rosa ate fried chicken.
2. Smelled good to eat.
3. Did Rosa find the rolls?
4. Rosa and Daniel?

5. Daniel picked up the basket.
6. In the basket.
7. Rosa wants an apple.
8. Potato salad.

▪ **Match each group of words in A with a group of
words in B to make a complete sentence. Write
the sentences below.**

A	B
The ants	looking for crumbs.
They were	marched in a row.
Rosa	saw them coming.
She moved	was for Daniel, not the ants.
The food	their blanket right away.

1. _____

2. _____

3. _____

4. _____

5. _____

> ■ Remember that a sentence is a group of words that tells or asks something. It stands for a complete thought.

■ **Choose the sentence in each pair of word groups below. Write the sentence.**

1. Katarina read about a car show. The big show.

   _____

2. She went to the car show. A most unusual car show.

   _____

3. Were very old models. Some cars were for the future.

   _____

4. How many cars were there? Cars at the show today?

   _____

5. Liked an old car best. Katarina liked an old car best.

   _____

6. Win a blue ribbon? Did it win a blue ribbon?

   _____

7. Yes, it won "Best of Show." "Best of Show."

   _____

■ **Read the paragraph below. Draw a line through each group of words that is not a sentence.**

Katarina drove to the car show. What did Katarina do there? Looked at different types of cars. Several judges looked at. Katarina and the judges liked the same car. They thought the old blue car looked like it was new. Felt it should win.

- Some sentences are **statements**. They tell something.
  EXAMPLE: Hawaii is a beautiful place to visit.
- Some sentences are **questions**. They ask something.
  EXAMPLE: Is Hawaii a beautiful place to visit?

- **Write S in front of each statement.
  Write Q in front of each question.**

_____ 1. Hawaii has many miles of beaches.

_____ 2. Does Hawaii have over a hundred islands?

_____ 3. The sun shines there on most days.

_____ 4. Many kinds of flowers grow in Hawaii.

_____ 5. Do farmers grow pineapples?

_____ 6. Sugar cane is an important crop in Hawaii.

_____ 7. Hawaii is called the Aloha State.

_____ 8. "Aloha" is a Hawaiian greeting.

_____ 9. Would you like to go to Hawaii?

_____ 10. When do you want to go?

- **Copy the sentences below. Underline the statement once. Underline the question twice.**

Many people visit Hawaii to ride the waves. Which beach do they like best?

_____

_____

_____

> - Some sentences are **commands**. They tell somebody to do something.
>   EXAMPLE: Squeeze all the juice out of the lemons.
> - Some sentences are **exclamations**. They show strong feelings or surprise.
>   EXAMPLE: What a sour taste that lemon has!

- **Write C in front of each command. Write E in front of each exclamation.**

_____ 1. How delicious those strawberries look!

_____ 2. Slice the bananas.

_____ 3. Add the water to the mix.

_____ 4. What a great lunch we'll have outside!

_____ 5. Clean the grill well.

_____ 6. How golden that chicken is!

_____ 7. Pass the salad, please.

_____ 8. The ants got the cake!

_____ 9. What a good idea this picnic was!

- **Write a sentence that is a command. Tell somebody to do the first step in making your favorite food.**

_____

- **Write a sentence that is an exclamation. Write what you would say after eating something that is good.**

_____

> - A sentence has two parts. One part is called the **subject**. The subject tells who or what the sentence is about. EXAMPLE: **The snow** is deep.

- **Underline the subject in each sentence.**

1. We went skiing today.
2. The snow was just right.
3. I flew down the hill.
4. Kamal lost his hat.
5. The hat was buried in the snow.

6. Skaters were on the pond.
7. The ice was smooth.
8. My son liked ice skating the best.
9. He skated very fast.
10. Our family watched him.

- **Complete each sentence by adding a subject.**

1. _____ put on her skis.

2. _____ helped his daughter.

3. _____ sat on the ski lift.

4. _____ went down the hill.

5. _____ was very cold.

6. _____ watched the snow fall.

7. _____ liked the snow.

8. _____ makes tracks in the snow.

9. _____ are on the slopes.

10. _____ can ski well.

11. _____ turned to the left.

12. _____ went home.

> ■ A sentence has two parts. One part is called the subject. The other part is called the **predicate**. The predicate tells what the subject is, was, or does.
>
> EXAMPLE: That big zoo **is nearby**.

■ **Underline the predicate in each sentence.**

1. John took his children to the zoo.
2. The lion cub growled at a bird.
3. The huge ape swung from a bar.
4. Barry liked the camels.
5. These tiny snakes are harmless.
6. Monkeys are fun to watch.
7. Vince fed an elephant.
8. Two elephants were in the pen.
9. Barbara saw the baby alligators.
10. They walked all around the zoo.

■ **Complete each sentence by adding a predicate.**

1. The chirping birds _____.

2. The children _____.

3. Barbara _____.

4. John _____.

5. A zookeeper _____.

6. The bears _____.

7. Vince _____.

8. Many people _____.

9. A sleeping bat _____.

10. The balloon man _____.

11. Everyone _____.

> - Two short sentences with the same predicate can be **combined** to make a new sentence. The two parts are joined by <u>and</u>.   EXAMPLE: Lou laughed. + Gina laughed. → Lou **and** Gina laughed.
> - Two short sentences with the same subject can be combined to make a new sentence. The two parts are joined by <u>and</u>.   EXAMPLE: Fred counted his money. + Fred paid for the tickets. → Fred counted his money **and** paid for the tickets.

- **Combine the sentences. Write the new sentence.**

1. Charlene got on the bus. The children got on the bus.

   _____

2. Bill stood in line for the tickets. His brother stood in line for the tickets.

   _____

3. Bill said good-bye to his brother. Bill picked up his suitcase.

   _____

4. He got on the bus. He sat next to Charlene.

   _____

5. Charlene read a book. Charlene played with the children.

   _____

6. Bill ate lunch. Bill wrote a letter.

   _____

7. The bus moved quickly. The bus arrived on time.

   _____

Combining Sentences

- Two short sentences that closely share an idea can be combined to make one sentence.
- The two sentences may be joined with connecting words such as <u>or</u>, <u>and</u>, or <u>but</u>. A comma is placed before these words.

  EXAMPLES: Tony found shells.
  + Amy caught seaweed. →
  Tony found shells, **and** Amy caught seaweed.
  I can't swim. + I can wade. →
  I can't swim, **but** I can wade.
  Fish from here. + Go to the dock. →
  Fish from here, **or** go to the dock.

- **Underline the two short sentences that were combined to make each sentence.**

  1. The wind howled, and the sand blew around.

  2. The people can swim, or they can sit on the beach.

  3. The water is cold, but the sand is warm.

  4. The sea is blue, and the foam is white.

  5. Rick carried our lunch, and we carried the chairs.

- **Combine the sentences using the word in ( ).**
  Write the new sentence.

  1. Take your towel. Lay it on the beach.   (and)

  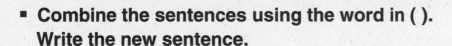
  _____

  2. You can walk in the sand. You can wade in the water.   (or)

  _____

  3. We can't use glass bottles on the beach. We can use plastic bottles.   (but)

  _____

> ■ If a sentence tells about more than one main idea, it should be rewritten as two sentences.
>
>   EXAMPLE: Most plants have seeds, some seeds are good to eat. → Most plants have seeds. Some seeds are good to eat.

■ **Read the sentences. Write two sentences for each.**

1. The seeds must be planted, this is done in many ways.

   _____

   _____

2. A seed floated in the breeze, it was very windy.

   _____

   _____

3. You can eat these seeds, Shameka will gather some more.

   _____

   _____

4. Birds and animals eat seeds, you can buy seeds for them in a store.

   _____

   _____

- **For each pair, underline the group of words that is a sentence.**

  1. Owls have large eyes. Catch food at night.

  2. Whales are. They live in the ocean.

  3. Lizards are reptiles. Are cold-blooded.

  4. What do chipmunks? Do you like chipmunks?

- **Write S in front of the statement. Write Q in front of the question.**

  _____ 1. Where did you go on your vacation?

  _____ 2. I went to Mexico.

  _____ 3. Did you take any photographs while you were there?

  _____ 4. No, I forgot my camera.

- **Write C in front of the command. Write E in front of the exclamation.**

  _____ 1. Give the cat its food.

  _____ 2. What beautiful fur your cat has!

  _____ 3. Don't let the cat go outside.

  _____ 4. Your cat is so playful!

- **Underline the subject. Circle the predicate.**

  1. The cat washed its face with its paw.

  2. Kirk threw a ball of yarn to the cat.

  3. The cat took a long nap.

  4. Kirk fed the cat after its nap.

- **Combine the sentences to make a new sentence.**

    1. Erin fed the baby. Erin put her in bed.

    _____

    _____

    2. Raul cleaned the house. Erin cleaned the house.

    _____

    _____

    3. Their friends were early. Raul and Erin were ready to greet them.

    _____

    _____

- **Read the sentences. Write two sentences for each.**

    1. My friend comes over, we go to see a movie.

    _____

    _____

    2. We stand in line, we get our tickets.

    _____

    _____

    3. We find a place to sit, we share some popcorn.

    _____

    _____

    4. The theater gets dark, the movie begins.

    _____

    _____

- **Rewrite the paragraph below, but make it less choppy. Combine each pair of sentences that is underlined. When you are finished, you will have five sentences in all.**

    Keiko is moving into a new apartment. It is much bigger than her old one. It is only a few miles away from her job. She has already moved most of her things. She cannot move her furniture. She has hired a moving company to take her furniture. The movers will be there at noon. She is excited. About moving.

_____

_____

_____

_____

_____

_____

_____

_____

_____

- **Write a paragraph about moving into a house or an apartment. Use at least two statements, one question, and one exclamation.**

_____

_____

_____

_____

_____

_____

- **Write a paragraph about your dream house or apartment. Use at least two statements, one question, and one exclamation.**

_____

_____

_____

_____

_____

_____

_____

> ▪ A **noun** is a word that names a person, place, or thing. The words <u>a</u>, <u>an</u>, and <u>the</u> are clues that show a noun is near.
>
> EXAMPLES: a pilot, the moon, an island

▪ **Underline the two nouns in each sentence.**

1. The astronaut looked out the window.

2. Clouds circled the earth.

3. The ocean looked like a lake.

4. Another astronaut ate her lunch.

5. An apple floated inside the cabin.

6. One man put on his spacesuit.

7. The astronaut walked in space.

8. The newspaper had pictures of him.

▪ **Write a noun from the box to complete each sentence.**

best	ocean	radio
cheer	happy	ship
day	hear	tall
doctor	over	the

1. They landed in the _____.

2. A _____ sailed over to them.

3. The _____ checked their health.

4. The news was on the _____.

5. We all yelled out a _____.

6. It was an exciting _____.

> - A **singular noun** names one person, place, or thing.
>   EXAMPLES: bee, fox, bench
> - A **plural noun** names more than one person, place, or thing. Add -s to most nouns to change them to mean more than one. Add -es to nouns that end with s, sh, ch, x, or z to change them to mean more than one.
>   EXAMPLES: bees, foxes, benches

- **Make the nouns plural.**

  1. skate _____

  2. car _____

  3. parade _____

  4. toe _____

  5. brush _____

  6. class _____

  7. inch _____

  8. box _____

  9. dish _____

  10. dollar _____

  11. leash _____

  12. watch _____

- **Rewrite each sentence. Choose the correct noun in ( ).**

  1. The fish are in a new (tank, tanks).

     _____

  2. All the (plant, plants) are fresh.

     _____

  3. The fish are hiding in those (castle, castles).

     _____

  4. Use that (net, nets) to catch the fish.

     _____

Common and Proper Nouns

> - A **proper noun** names a particular person, place, or thing. It begins with a capital letter.
>   EXAMPLES: Mel Gibson, London, Park School
> - A **common noun** does not name a particular person, place, or thing.
>   EXAMPLES: actor, city, school

- **Write C for a common noun. Write P for a proper noun.**

_____ 1. girl

_____ 2. Mexico

_____ 3. mountain

_____ 4. country

_____ 5. Alabama

_____ 6. Tolman Company

_____ 7. lake

_____ 8. Helen Keller

_____ 9. Friday

_____ 10. Mojave Desert

_____ 11. building

_____ 12. doctor

- **Read the sentences. Draw one line under the common noun. Circle the proper noun.**

1. The ocean was very rough on Tuesday.

2. The waves pounded Sand Beach.

3. The beach is in Mexico.

4. Some people were there from Portland.

5. Julio spied a seaplane.

6. Koji saw a Flying Eagle.

7. The plane was flying to Canada.

8. Sarah waved to the pilot.

> ■ A **verb** usually shows action. It tells what a person, place, or thing is or was doing.
> EXAMPLES: The cub **sleeps** in the shade.
> A tiger **ran** across the field.

■ **Underline the verb in each sentence.**

1. Jeannette took a trip to Africa.

2. She flew there in a plane.

3. A beautiful bird chattered in the forest.

4. Elephants drank from the stream.

5. An animal leaped in the air.

■ **Choose a verb from the box to complete each sentence.**

| buzz | grow | roar | search | swing |

1. The lions _____ loudly.

2. Many plants _____ by the stream.

3. Monkeys _____ from branches.

4. The insects _____ above Jeanette.

5. She will _____ for butterflies.

■ **Use an action verb in a sentence about animals in Africa.**

_____

- Verbs can show that an action happens in the **present**.
  EXAMPLE: The game **starts** now.
- Verbs in the present used with singular subjects end in -s.   EXAMPLE: Troy **likes** to pitch.
- Verbs in the present used with plural subjects have no special endings.   EXAMPLE: The people **watch** the game.

- **Complete each sentence with the correct verb.**

1. Tran _____ to America. (move, moves)

2. His family _____ in Asia. (live, lives)

3. Tran's friends _____ him find an apartment. (help, helps)

4. His neighbor _____ him about an English class. (tell, tells)

5. Tran _____ how to speak English. (learn, learns)

6. Two other students _____ Tran to a party. (invite, invites)

7. They _____ about their new life in America. (talk, talks)

8. Tran _____ talking with his new friends. (enjoy, enjoys)

- **Write sentences with verbs in the present.**

1. Tell something about the place where you live.

   _____

   _____

2. Tell something you like about the place where you live.

   _____

   _____

> - Verbs can show that an action happened in the **past**.
>   Add the endings -d or -ed to most verbs to show that
>   something happened in the past.
>   EXAMPLE: Yesterday we **washed** our cars.

- **Underline the verb in each sentence. Write P in
  front of each sentence with a verb in the past.**

  _____ 1. My friends and I like to jog in the park.

  _____ 2. We turned left on the trail.

  _____ 3. They stopped at the water fountain.

  _____ 4. I waited in the shade.

  _____ 5. We jog for a long time.

  _____ 6. They rested for a half hour.

- **Rewrite the sentences. Change each verb from
  the present to the past by adding -d or -ed.**

  1. My friends and I enter the five-mile race.

  _____

  2. We start the race together.

  _____

  3. We walk up a steep hill.

  _____

  4. I hope to win.

  _____

  5. I finish in first place.

  _____

> - A **linking verb** does not show action. It links, or joins, the subject to a word in the predicate. Verbs such as am, is, are, was, and were are linking verbs.
>   EXAMPLES: Those insects **are** crickets.
>   They **were** noisy.

- **Write L in front of each sentence that has a linking verb.**

_____ 1. The crickets are loud tonight.

_____ 2. They chirp in the grass.

_____ 3. The dogs bark at the cars.

_____ 4. They were quiet earlier.

_____ 5. An owl screeches in the tree.

_____ 6. It is afraid of the dogs.

_____ 7. The white cat meows at her kitten.

_____ 8. She tells it not to wander.

_____ 9. The birds are asleep in their nests.

_____ 10. A jet roars over the house.

_____ 11. Everyone is quiet inside.

_____ 12. Just listen to the sounds at night!

- **Use a linking verb in a sentence that tells about another sound you can hear at night.**

_____

> - Use <u>am</u> with the word I.
>   EXAMPLE: I **am** ready to go fishing.
> - Use <u>is</u> with one person, place, or thing.
>   EXAMPLE: Joe **is** ready to go, too.
> - Use <u>are</u> with more than one and with the word <u>you</u>.
>   EXAMPLES: We **are** all ready now.
>   **Are** you ready to go?

■ **Write <u>am</u>, <u>is</u>, or <u>are</u>.**

Some friends _____ fishing. Joe _____ the first to

catch a fish.

He says, "It _____ too small. I will put it back into the

water. When it _____ older, I might catch it again!"

"You _____ smart," says Mary. "It _____ good to

throw fish back when they are too small."

"I _____ sure I have something big!" shouts Sam.

Mary and Joe watch Sam pull the fish to the bank.

"That _____ not a fish," says Mary. She holds up an old

tin can. "People spoil our fishing spot with junk. I _____

ready to put up a 'No Dumping' sign here."

"There _____ two signs here already," says Sam. "They

_____ over there behind that pile of junk!"

- Use <u>was</u> and <u>were</u> to tell about the past.
- Use <u>was</u> with one person, place, or thing.
  EXAMPLE: Chris **was** busy in the kitchen.
- Use <u>were</u> with more than one and with the word <u>you</u>.
  EXAMPLES: The dishes **were** in the sink.
  We were glad that you **were** here to help.

- **Write <u>was</u> or <u>were</u>.**

1. Ben _____ making a tree house for his children.

2. He _____ working in the back yard.

3. The boards _____ too long.

4. The saw _____ sharp.

5. Ben _____ using the saw to cut the boards.

6. Then he _____ looking for the nails.

7. Where _____ the nails?

8. They _____ behind the boards.

9. Ben _____ careful when he used the hammer.

10. Finally, all of the boards _____ nailed in place.

11. Then Ben _____ ready to paint the tree house.

12. There _____ several colors he could use.

13. The children _____ excited about their new tree house.

14. But the paint _____ not dry yet.

15. They _____ going to have to wait to use the tree house.

> - A **helping verb** helps the main verb. <u>Have</u>, <u>has</u>, or <u>had</u> helps a main verb show action in the past.
>
>   EXAMPLES: Rita has moved to a cottage.
>
>   They have packed their bags.
>
>   The farmer had milked the goat.

- **Underline the helping verb. Circle the main verb.**

1. The sun has risen.

2. The roosters had remembered to crow.

3. The cows have chewed the grass.

4. Rita had collected the eggs.

5. Ben has baked some fresh bread.

6. We have eaten breakfast.

- **Rewrite the sentences using the correct verb in ( ).**

1. I (has, have) walked to the park.

   _____

2. A gentle rain (has, have) started.

   _____

3. It (has, had) rained yesterday.

   _____

4. Pat (has, had) bought an umbrella last week.

   _____

- Use <u>does</u> with a singular subject to show the present.
  EXAMPLE: Anna **does** all the costumes.
- Use <u>do</u> with I, <u>you</u>, and plural subjects to show the present.
  EXAMPLE: Alan and Lyn **do** want to see the play.
- Use <u>did</u> without a helping verb to show the past.
  EXAMPLE: Ed **did** act in the play.
- Use <u>done</u> with a helping verb to show the past.
  EXAMPLE: Jenna has **done** her part.

- **Underline the correct verb.**

1. (Do, Does) Henry and Andrea have a savings account here?

2. Yes, they (does, do).

3. Henry (do, does) put some money into the account each month.

- Use <u>sees</u> with a singular subject to show the present.
  EXAMPLE: Anna **sees** a runner.
- Use <u>see</u> with I, <u>you</u>, and plural subjects to show the present.
  EXAMPLE: Alan and Lyn **see** the first runners.
- Use <u>saw</u> without a helping verb to show the past.
  EXAMPLE: Ed **saw** the high jump contest.
- Use <u>seen</u> with a helping verb to show the past.
  EXAMPLE: Jenna has **seen** many track meets.

- **Underline the correct verb.**

1. We went to the track meet because my friends had (seen, saw) an ad.

2. Rajiv said, "I (see, sees) our seats."

3. Today the three of us (saw, seen) several different events.

> - Use <u>gives</u> with a singular subject to show the present.
>   EXAMPLE: Anna **gives** the actors a gift.
> - Use <u>give</u> with <u>I</u>, <u>you</u>, and plural subjects to show the present.
>   EXAMPLE: Alan and Lyn **give** tips to the actors.
> - Use <u>gave</u> without a helping verb to show the past.
>   EXAMPLE: Ed **gave** a speech before the play.
> - Use <u>given</u> with a helping verb to show the past.
>   EXAMPLE: Jenna had **given** a speech last year.

- **Underline the correct verb.**

1. Our friends (gave, given) us a map.

2. The map was (gave, given) to them last year.

3. It (give, gives) us information about the city.

4. Now I have (gave, given) the map to Carmen.

> - Use <u>goes</u> with a singular subject to show the present.
>   EXAMPLE: Anna **goes** to the museum.
> - Use <u>go</u> with <u>I</u>, <u>you</u>, and plural subjects to show the present.
>   EXAMPLE: Alan and Lyn **go** to the museum often.
> - Use <u>went</u> without a helping verb to show the past.
>   EXAMPLE: Ed **went** to the museum last week.
> - Use <u>gone</u> with a helping verb to show the past.
>   EXAMPLE: Jenna had **gone** with Ed.

- **Underline the correct verb.**

1. We (go, goes) to the museum.

2. Sue (go, goes) with her neighbor.

3. I have (gone, went) there before.

4. Sue (go, goes) there often.

5. Ann and Jeff (go, goes) there, too.

6. Tim (went, gone) last year.

7. We always (go, goes) in the spring.

8. You have (gone, went) with us.

- A **pronoun** is a word that takes the place of a noun.
- Pronouns that take the place of singular nouns are
  I, me, you, he, him, she, her, and it.
    - EXAMPLE: **Dave** ate slowly. **He** ate slowly.
- Pronouns that take the place of plural nouns are we, us,
  you, they, and them.
    - EXAMPLE: The popcorn is for **the guests**.
    - The popcorn is for **them**.

- **Choose the correct pronoun in ( ) to take the place
  of the underlined noun. Then rewrite the sentences.**

  1. Maria invited friends over to watch a movie.   (they, them)

  _____

  2. Maria made popcorn for her friends.   (She, They)

  _____

  3. Hot air tosses popcorn around.   (it, them)

  _____

  4. Anthony put salt on his popcorn.   (He, They)

  _____

  5. Don gave some popcorn to Colleen.   (her, them)

  _____

  6. Sue passed the bowl to Alex and Rob.   (it, them)

  _____

- **Write two sentences using pronouns.**

  1. _____

  2. _____

> - Use these pronouns as **subjects**: I, you, he, she, it, we, and they.   EXAMPLE: **I** like mysteries.
> - Use these pronouns as **objects** that follow an action verb: me, you, him, her, it, us, and them.
>   EXAMPLE: Sherlock Holmes amazed **them**.

- **Write S if the underlined pronoun is used as a subject. Write O if it is used as an object.**

_____ 1. She gave him two mysteries.

_____ 2. He read both of them.

_____ 3. They were about Sherlock Holmes.

_____ 4. He thanked her for the books.

_____ 5. He said they were both wonderful.

_____ 6. She said he could borrow any other books he wanted.

- **Rewrite the sentences using a pronoun from the box in place of the underlined words.**

He   them   us   We

1. Jesse and I went to the rodeo.

_____

2. One woman roped two calves.

_____

3. Jesse couldn't believe her strength.

_____

4. The woman gave Jesse and me a smile when she won.

_____

> ▪ A **possessive pronoun** is a pronoun that shows who or what owns something. The pronouns <u>my</u>, <u>our</u>, <u>your</u>, <u>his</u>, <u>her</u>, <u>its</u>, and <u>their</u> are possessive pronouns.
> EXAMPLE: Janet drove **her** car to work.

▪ **Underline the possessive pronoun in each sentence.**

1. Two workers were late for their jobs.

2. Their names were Peg and Mike.

3. Our boss will not be happy.

4. Peg put her time card in the clock.

5. Mike answered his telephone.

6. Peg wants to know when we have our lunch break.

▪ **Write the correct possessive pronoun in each blank.**

1. Bill lives in a house. _____ house is white.

2. I live in an apartment. _____ apartment has two bedrooms.

3. Sarah lives on a farm. _____ farm is very large.

4. During the summer, Tom and Donna live on a houseboat.

   _____ houseboat goes up and down the river.

5. My family has one car. _____ car is old.

6. You have a new dress. _____ dress is blue and white.

7. The tree is big. _____ branches are long and thick.

8. Julio has a brother. _____ brother's name is Arturo.

- Use I in the subject of a sentence.
  EXAMPLE: **I** took Sara bowling.
- Use me in the predicate of a sentence.
  EXAMPLE: Bev was waiting for **me**.
- Use I or me when naming yourself and others.
  EXAMPLES: Inez and **I** like to go bowling.
  Inez saw Ming and **me** at the bowling alley.

- **Complete the sentences with the words in ( ).**
  Be sure to put the words in the correct order.

1. _____ and _____ wanted to go bowling.   (Karen, I)

2. Some of our friends were waiting for _____ and

   _____.   (me, her)

3. Sally went with _____ and _____.   (me, Karen)

4. _____ and _____ had a great time.   (Sally, I)

5. Sally had bowled with _____ and _____
   before.   (me, Carlos)

6. _____ and _____ helped our friend Karen learn
   how to bowl.   (I, Sally)

7. Karen smiled at _____ and _____.   (me, Sally)

8. _____ and _____ saw that Karen was going to like
   bowling.   (Sally, I)

9. Karen thanked _____ and _____ for teaching her how
   to bowl.   (me, Sally)

10. _____ and _____ were glad we could help.   (I, Sally)

Lesson 35

Adjectives

> ■ An **adjective** is a word that describes a noun or a pronoun. It tells which one, how many, or what kind.
> EXAMPLE: The **two** clocks made a **loud** ring.

■ **Underline the adjectives.**

1. The bright sunlight peeked through the window.

2. The noisy alarm woke me up.

3. It was going to be a great day.

4. I threw on my clean clothes.

5. Three friends met me for lunch.

6. One friend told a funny story.

7. She made a strange face.

8. I had a great time.

■ **Complete the sentences with adjectives from the box.**

big	empty	little	crowded
brown	first	muddy	white
cold	gold	new	clean
deep	happy	red	old

1. After lunch, we walked through a _____ crowd at the

   _____ store.

2. It had rained so my _____ shoes got _____.

3. The store was _____ , but we were _____.

4. I bought a _____ ring and a _____ shirt.

> - Add -er to most adjectives to compare two persons, places, or things.
>   EXAMPLE: The car was **smaller** than the truck.
> - Add -est to most adjectives to compare more than two persons, places, or things.
>   EXAMPLE: That is the **smallest** car I've seen.

- **Underline the correct form of the adjective in each sentence.**

1. This is the (stranger, strangest) weather we have ever had.

2. It is much (cooler, coolest) today than it was yesterday.

3. Tuesday was the (hotter, hottest) day of the week.

4. It is usually (rainier, rainiest) in the spring than in the summer.

5. However, this spring was (drier, driest) than last spring.

6. This year it rained a (greater, greatest) amount in the summer than it did in the spring.

- **Add -er or -est to the underlined adjectives. Write the new words.**

1. Tornadoes are the big weather problem we have. _____

2. They are hard to predict than thunderstorms. _____

3. Some tornadoes come close to the ground than others. _____

4. In some areas, hurricanes are a great threat than

   tornadoes. _____

5. Hurricane winds are calm in the eye of the storm. _____

6. During a storm, emergency crews often have to

   work long hours. _____

> ▪ Use <u>a</u> before words that begin with a consonant sound.
>   EXAMPLES: a child, a fresh egg
> ▪ Use <u>an</u> before words that begin with a vowel sound.
>   EXAMPLES: an adult, an old egg

▪ **Write <u>a</u> or <u>an</u>.**

1. _____ barn
2. _____ apple
3. _____ dentist
4. _____ tree
5. _____ address
6. _____ chair
7. _____ doctor
8. _____ bedroom
9. _____ door
10. _____ house

11. _____ old barn
12. _____ red apple
13. _____ good dentist
14. _____ apple tree
15. _____ home address
16. _____ orange chair
17. _____ doctor's office
18. _____ upstairs bedroom
19. _____ open door
20. _____ unusual house

▪ **Write <u>a</u> or <u>an</u> to complete this paragraph.**

_____ police officer came to the scene of _____ accident.

_____ automobile had hit _____ truck. But it was not _____

emergency. Neither driver had _____ injury. The police

officer filed _____ report.

> - An **adverb** is a word that describes a verb. It tells how, when, or where. Many adverbs end in -ly.
>   EXAMPLES: The man walked **slowly**. **How?**
>   The man walked **today**. **When?**
>   The man walked **there**. **Where?**

carefully	now	far	then
later	everywhere	quietly	here
early	quickly	happily	out

- **The words above are adverbs. Write each word under a heading below to show if the word tells how, when, or where.**

How?	When?	Where?
_____	_____	_____
_____	_____	_____
_____	_____	_____
_____	_____	_____

- **Underline each adverb. Write how, when, or where.**

1. Shawn eats breakfast early.   _____

2. Andy walked quietly.   _____

3. We will eat later.   _____

4. The bird flew there.   _____

> - Use the adjective <u>good</u> to mean "better than average."
>   EXAMPLE: We had a **good** time.
> - Use the adverb <u>well</u> to mean "in a good way."
>   EXAMPLE: No one slept very **well**.

- **Write <u>good</u> or <u>well</u>.**

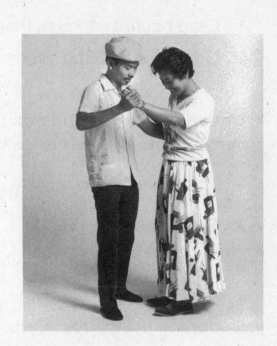

1. We saw a _____ movie last week.

2. Isabel danced very _____.

3. Everyone had a _____ time.

4. Lisa knows how to bake quite _____.

5. She made _____ bread for us.

6. I read a really _____ book last week.

7. It was written very _____.

- **Use <u>good</u> or <u>well</u> correctly in this paragraph.**

Benjamin did not have a _____ time when he was ill.

But the doctor did his job _____ . Soon Benjamin

was _____ enough to return to work. He said it was

_____ to be back. All the other workers were glad

Benjamin was _____ . They really missed his _____

sense of humor. He has always told jokes very _____ . He

is a _____ friend to everyone.

- **Underline the singular nouns. Circle the plural nouns.**

    1. The garden will be full of flowers.
    2. The family will mow the yard.
    3. The roses are in the sun.
    4. The birds love the birdbath.

- **Underline the common nouns. Circle the proper nouns.**

    1. Greg bought seeds at Plant World.
    2. Greg scattered the seeds.
    3. He waters his plants every Monday.
    4. We'll have corn in July.

- **Underline the action verb. Circle the linking verbs. Write <u>present</u> or <u>past</u> on the lines.**

    1. The daisies grow quickly. _____
    2. The roses were droopy. _____
    3. The pansies are colorful. _____

- **Underline the correct verb.**

    1. A bee (rests, rest) in a flower.
    2. I (am, is, are) happy about the garden.
    3. It (were, was) raining yesterday.
    4. I (sees, see, seen) some new flowers.
    5. A garden (do, done, does) take time to grow.
    6. I (gone, goes, go) to the garden every day.

- **Underline the correct helping verb.**

    1. The family (has, have) moved.
    2. Doug (have, has) started his new job.
    3. His children (has, have) made some new friends.

▪ Underline the correct pronoun.

1. (She, Her) took a trip.

2. This is (her, she) ticket.

3. Mary and (I, me) were gone for a week.

4. We were in (we, our) hotel room.

5. (Me, My) suitcase got lost.

6. Did Sheryl go with (their, them)?

▪ Underline each adjective that compares.

1. This leaf is the darkest on the twig.

2. The twig is shorter than the branch.

3. Can you reach the lowest branch?

4. Your motorcycle is older than my motorcycle.

5. My motorcycle is cleaner than your motorcycle.

6. Our motorcycles are the greatest in the world.

▪ Underline the adverbs.

1. The carrots grew quickly.

2. The rain is falling softly.

3. We'll have blossoms soon.

4. The sun shines brightly.

5. The wind blows quietly.

6. The soil is very rich.

▪ Write good or well.

1. Dan slept _____ .

2. He feels _____ rested.

3. He puts on his _____ pants.

4. He interviews for a _____ job.

5. He wants to do _____.

6. Dan had a _____ day.

- **The underlined words in the paragraph below are wrong. Rewrite the paragraph correctly.**

    Scott is driving to work by himself. He left <u>earliest</u> than usual to get ready for a big meeting. He is making <u>well</u> time. Then suddenly the cars <u>is</u> moving <u>slowest</u> than before. Scott <u>need</u> to be at work on time. <u>Our</u> has many things to do before his meeting. The meeting <u>are</u> at eight o'clock. Now all the cars <u>has</u> stopped. Scott <u>look</u> all around, but <u>him</u> does not see a problem. Finally, the cars <u>starts</u> moving again. Scott thinks this is the <u>sillier</u> thing he has ever seen. What <u>were</u> the cause of this traffic jam? Scott <u>have</u> no idea!

_____

_____

_____

_____

_____

_____

_____

_____

_____

_____

- **Write a funny paragraph describing something that has happened to you lately. Then go back and circle two singular or plural nouns, two common or proper nouns, an action verb, a helping verb, two pronouns, three adjectives, and two adverbs. If you don't have all of these, add them to your paragraph.**

_____

_____

_____

_____

_____

_____

_____

_____

_____

_____

_____

_____

_____

_____

_____

_____

- Use a **capital letter** to begin proper nouns, such as days of the week, months, or holidays.
  EXAMPLES: Monday, Friday, February, May, Thanksgiving, Canada Day
- Use a **small letter** to begin the name of each season.
  EXAMPLES: spring, summer, fall, winter

- **Rewrite the words. Use capital letters where they are needed.**

1. mother's day _____

2. winter _____

3. july _____

4. saturday _____

5. june _____

6. spring _____

7. thursday _____

8. april _____

- **Rewrite the sentences. Use capital letters where they are needed.**

1. This winter I am going to a parade on new year's day.

_____

_____

2. The parade is in january.

_____

3. It is on saturday.

_____

4. Last summer I went to a parade on labor day.

_____

_____

> - Use a capital letter to begin each word in proper nouns, such as names of people, family names, and place names.
>   EXAMPLES: Gary Woodlawn, Grandma Cary, London, Vermont
> - Use a small letter to begin a family name that comes after words like my, your, and their.
>   EXAMPLES: their uncle, my mother

- **Rewrite the words. Use capital letters where they are needed.**

1. uncle brian _____
2. new york _____
3. jamie smith _____
4. my father _____
5. dallas _____

6. florida _____
7. aunt sue _____
8. charles _____
9. france _____
10. montreal _____

- **Rewrite the sentences. Use capital letters where they are needed.**

1. Our theater group put on a play about nelson mandela.

_____

2. Did your uncle from san diego see it?

_____

3. I think aunt sarah liked it.

_____

4. susan allen had the part of winnie mandela.

_____

> ■ Use a capital letter to begin the first word of a sentence.
> EXAMPLE: We are having a family reunion.

■ **Write the sentences. Use a capital letter to begin each sentence.**

1. have you ever had a family reunion?

   _____

2. no, but it sounds like fun.

   _____

3. we are having our reunion in Lincoln, Nebraska.

   _____

4. elena is sending out the invitations next week.

   _____

5. she hopes that more than 200 people will attend.

   _____

6. our family lives all across North America.

   _____

7. it will be exciting to meet some relatives we don't know.

   _____

8. will it be difficult to find everyone?

   _____

9. i am not sure.

   _____

> - Use a **period** (.) at the end of a sentence that tells something.
>   EXAMPLE: Ron has a new guppy**.**
> - Use a **question mark** (?) at the end of a sentence that asks a question.
>   EXAMPLE: Did he name it**?**
> - Use an **exclamation point** (!) at the end of a sentence that shows strong feelings.
>   EXAMPLE: What a good swimmer it is**!**

- **Use a period, question mark, or exclamation point at the end of each sentence.**

    1. Guppies can live in a large bowl of water
    2. Does the water need to be cleaned
    3. Look at their pretty colors
    4. How many are there
    5. What a big tail that guppy has

- **Write the sentences. End each one with a period, question mark, or exclamation point.**

    1. Do you feed guppies dry food

       _____

    2. I can't believe how well they swim

       _____

    3. The biggest guppy is named Butch

       _____

    4. What is the little one's name

       _____

    5. I like him the best

       _____

> - An **abbreviation** is the shortened form of a word.
> - Use a capital letter to begin an abbreviation for a title of respect or an abbreviation for the name of a place. Use a period at the end of these abbreviations.
>   EXAMPLES: Ms., Mrs., Mr., Dr., Yellow Brick Rd.
> - An **initial** is the first letter of a name. Capitalize an initial and put a period after it.
>   EXAMPLE: M. C. Livingston for Molly Coe Livingston

- **Write the names. Correct the initials and the abbreviations that are underlined. Use capital letters and periods where they are needed.**

  1. Arthur c Clarke _____

  2. mrs Tolan _____

  3. Cherry Tree rd _____

  4. dr Spock _____

  5. a a Milne _____

  6. ms t Lowry _____

  7. Quimby st _____

  8. mr Stephen King _____

  9. e m Thomas _____

- **Circle the mistakes in the sentence below. Write each correction on a line.**

  mr Tom Sawyer is in a book by m Twain.

  1. _____   2. _____

> ▪ Use capital letters to begin abbreviations for days of the week. Use periods at the end of the abbreviations.
>   EXAMPLES: Sun., Mon., Wed., Thurs., Sat.
> ▪ Use capital letters to begin abbreviations for months of the year. Use periods at the end of the abbreviations.
>   EXAMPLES: Jan., Feb., Apr., Aug., Nov., Dec.

▪ **Write the abbreviations for the days and the months. Use capital letters and periods where they are needed.**

1. Thursday _____

2. August _____

3. Sunday _____

4. March _____

5. Tuesday _____

6. February _____

7. Monday _____

8. September _____

9. October _____

10. Saturday _____

11. December _____

12. Wednesday _____

13. November _____

14. Friday _____

15. January _____

16. April _____

▪ **Circle the mistakes in the sentences below. Write each correction on a line.**

1. That bill must be paid by sat, sept 4th.

   _____   _____

2. I have a doctor's appointment on fri, oct 31st.

   _____   _____

- Use a **comma** (,) after the words <u>yes</u> and <u>no</u> if they begin a sentence.   EXAMPLES: Yes, I saw the parade downtown. No, I didn't go to the dance.
- Use a comma to separate three or more items listed together in a sentence.   EXAMPLE: The float was red, white, and blue.

- **Write the sentences. Use commas where they are needed.**

1. Yes the band was in the parade.

   _____

2. Patty Carlos and Jo rode on a float.

   _____

3. We saw the floats clowns and marching bands.

   _____

4. The horses fire engines and flags came next.

   _____

5. No I didn't stay until the end.

   _____

6. Yes I wanted to stay.

   _____

7. We bought juice nuts and fruit to eat.

   _____

8. Yes I had a good time.

   _____

9. Patty Carlos Jo and I rode home together.

   _____

Lesson 47

- Use a comma between numbers for the day and year in the **heading** of a letter.   EXAMPLE: June 26, 2006
- Use a comma between the city and state in an **address**. EXAMPLE: Carbondale, Illinois 62901
- Use a capital letter to begin the first word and all names in the **greeting** of a letter. Use a comma at the end of the greeting.   EXAMPLE: Dear Stephanie,
- Use a capital letter to begin only the first word in the **closing** of a letter. Use a comma at the end of the closing.   EXAMPLE: Very truly yours,

- **Circle the words that should be capitalized in the letter. Add commas where needed.**

34 High Rise Street
New York New York 10011
April 3, 2006

dear gina

uuu uuuuu uu uuu uuuuu uuuuu uu uuuuuuu uuuu uuu uuuuuu uu uu uuuu uuuu.

your friend

Danielle

- **Rewrite these parts of a letter. Use capital letters and commas where they are needed.**

1. May 7, 2006 _____

2. Miami Florida 33137 _____

3. dear alicia _____   4. with love _____

- Add an **apostrophe** (') and -s ('s) to nouns like girl to show that one person owns something.
  EXAMPLE: the **girl's** present
- Add an apostrophe after nouns like girls to show that more than one person owns something.
  EXAMPLE: the **girls'** presents
- Add an apostrophe and -s ('s) to plural nouns like children to show that more than one person owns something.   EXAMPLE: the **children's** presents

- **Rewrite each phrase to show ownership. Add an apostrophe or an apostrophe and -s to the underlined words.**

1. the pilot hat
_____

2. the woman car
_____

3. five dogs bones
_____

4. a kitten toys
_____

5. a golfer hat
_____

6. many mens hats
_____

7. the women cars
_____

8. a worker contract
_____

9. ten violins strings
_____

10. the birds nests
_____

- **Write a sentence telling about something that belongs to a friend or friends. Use an apostrophe or an apostrophe and -s to show who owns it.**

_____

_____

> - A **contraction** is a word made by joining two words.
> - Use an apostrophe to show that letters are left out.
>   EXAMPLES: **it's** = it is   **hasn't** = has not

- **Write contractions for the pairs of words. Leave out the letters that are underlined.**

1. she + <u>i</u>s _____

2. we + <u>a</u>re _____

3. you + <u>wi</u>ll _____

4. I + <u>ha</u>ve _____

5. he + <u>woul</u>d _____

6. she + <u>ha</u>s _____

- **Write contractions for the pairs of words.**

1. has + not _____

2. is + not _____

3. were + not _____

4. I + will _____

5. that + is _____

6. would + not _____

7. they + will _____

8. there + is _____

- **Rewrite the sentences. Use contractions for the words that are underlined.**

1. Jay <u>has not</u> seen that movie.

   _____

2. <u>It is</u> about a strange land.

   _____

3. One year winter <u>does not</u> come.

   _____

4. The people <u>do not</u> mind.

   _____

> - Use **quotation marks** (" ") before and after the words a speaker says.   EXAMPLE: Miranda said, "I'm going to leave for about an hour."
> - Use a comma between the words the speaker says and the rest of the sentence. Put the comma before the quotation marks. Capitalize the first word the speaker says.   EXAMPLES: "We're leaving now," said Miranda. **or** Miranda said, "We're leaving now."

- **Read the cartoon. Think about who is talking and what that person is saying.**

- **Answer the questions about the cartoon. Use quotation marks and commas where needed.**

1. What did Carl say first?

_____

2. What did Jane say first?

_____

3. What did Jane say about the receipts?

_____

4. What was the last thing Carl said?

_____

- **Correct the sentences. Circle letters that should be capitalized. Put periods, question marks, exclamation points, and commas where they are needed.**

1. mr and mrs kamp lived in a house on may street

2. one saturday the couple cleaned the attic

3. ellen found an old letter from dr r m wilson

4. the letter came all the way from japan

5. peter found a picture of roses daisies and tulips

6. did aunt julia take that photo on valentine's day

7. no uncle george took the photo last april

8. what a mess the attic is

9. yes ellen will clean out the attic next spring

- **Rewrite the abbreviations. Use capital letters and periods where needed.**

1. tues _____

2. fri _____

3. mrs _____

4. elm st _____

5. dec _____

6. m c lee _____

7. apr _____

8. j r adams _____

9. feb _____

10. mon _____

11. smith rd _____

12. mr _____

13. sat _____

14. dr a roberts _____

15. ms n lincoln _____

16. aug _____

- **Add commas to these parts of a letter. Circle the small letters that should be capital letters.**

  1. birmingham alabama 35205
  2. august 18 2006
  3. dear kim
  4. yours truly
  5. dear mom
  6. austin texas 78753
  7. sincerely
  8. dear dr. west
  9. your friend
  10. dec. 1 2006
  11. glendora california 91741
  12. with love

- **Add apostrophes, quotation marks, and commas to these sentences where they are needed.**

  1. This is Ellens recipe said Louisa.
  2. Louisa said Its her childrens favorite.
  3. Id like to try to make that recipe said Mike.
  4. Mike takes out the chicken cheese noodles and spices.
  5. This recipe doesnt look hard to make Mike said.
  6. Lets read the recipe together said Louisa.
  7. She asked Are the directions printed on the back of the card?
  8. Mike said Yes theyre on the back.
  9. He said Ill grate the cheese first.
  10. Mikes apron is untied so Louisa reties it.
  11. Mike doesnt know where the large baking dish is.
  12. Louisa says shell help him look in a minute.

■ **Correct the story. As you read it, circle letters that should be capitals. Put periods, question marks, exclamation points, commas, apostrophes, and quotation marks where they are needed. Rewrite the title and the story on the lines.**

A Hidden Surprise

ms andersons cat is named sam _____ what a big smart

beautiful cat he is _____ one summer day ms anderson

couldnt find him _____ do you know where he was _____

he was under the porch with three new kittens _____ ms

anderson said your name is samantha now _____

_____

_____

_____

_____

_____

_____

_____

_____

_____

- **Write a letter to Ms. Anderson. Tell her about something that surprised you. Use your address and today's date in the heading. Write a greeting and a closing. Be sure to use an abbreviation and a contraction in your letter. Use capital letters, periods, question marks, exclamation points, commas, and apostrophes. Check your letter for any mistakes.**

> - A **sentence** must tell a complete thought.
> - Remember to begin a sentence with a capital letter and end it with a period, a question mark, or an exclamation point.
>   EXAMPLE: **Thought:** having friends over for dinner
>   **Sentence:** I am having friends over for dinner.

- **Write each of these thoughts about making lasagna as a sentence.**

1. buying some ground beef

_____

2. using one box of noodles

_____

3. boiling water for the noodles

_____

4. pouring one can of tomato sauce

_____

5. sprinkling one teaspoon of oregano

_____

6. grating $\frac{1}{4}$ cup of parmesan cheese

_____

7. cracking one egg

_____

8. stirring in one small carton of cottage cheese

_____

9. cooking the lasagna

_____

- A **paragraph** is a group of sentences about one main idea. **Indent** the first line. To indent a paragraph, leave a space before the first word.
- A paragraph should have sentences about the same subject.

  EXAMPLE:

  Last night I made a list of all the things I still needed for my lasagna recipe. Then I went to the store. I bought some ground beef, tomato sauce, parmesan cheese, and a small container of cottage cheese.

- **Read the paragraph. Then write another paragraph. Tell what else you could make for a dinner with some friends. Be sure to indent.**

  I decided to cook lasagna. First, I browned the ground beef in a skillet. Next, I cooked the beef in the sauce. I put the pasta noodles in a large pot of boiling water. Then I combined the egg with the cottage cheese and parmesan cheese. I made the lasagna with layers of noodles, meat sauce, cheese mixture, and mozzarella cheese.

_____

_____

_____

_____

_____

_____

- A **topic sentence** tells the main idea, or topic, of a paragraph.
- All sentences in a paragraph should be about that topic.
  EXAMPLE: <u>There are many safety rules you should follow when cooking.</u> Turn the handles of pots and pans on the stove away from you to avoid accidentally knocking them over. Use oven mitts to handle hot cooking tools. Keep baking soda nearby to put out any fires that might start.

- **Underline the topic sentence in each paragraph.**

It is important to plan ahead when you are preparing a dinner for friends. Decide what foods you will make. Read through the recipes. Make a list of the ingredients you need. Then buy them at the store. Allow plenty of time for each recipe.

_____

Set the table before your guests arrive. Place the napkin and the fork to the left of the plate. Put the knife and the spoon to the right of the plate. Set the glass above the tip of the knife. You can put a centerpiece, such as flowers, on the table. Be sure that your guests can see over it.

_____

Cooking a variety of recipes can help you learn about different cultures. People from all over the world live in North America. They have brought recipes that use many ingredients and spices.

> ▪ **Details** after the topic sentence in a paragraph should tell more about the main idea.
>
> EXAMPLE: There are many safety rules you should follow when cooking. <u>Turn the handles of pots and pans on the stove away from you to avoid accidentally knocking them over.</u> <u>Use oven mitts to handle hot cooking tools.</u> <u>Keep baking soda nearby to put out any fires that might start.</u>

▪ **Circle the topic sentence. Underline the three sentences that give details about the main idea. Write the circled and underlined sentences in a new paragraph.**

You can make punch look more festive for a party. My friend is a chef in a restaurant. One way is to put whole cloves in the center of orange, lemon, or lime slices. Some people prefer to drink soda at a party. Then float the fruit slices on top of the punch. Or you may wish to add a fruit-filled ice ring or fruit-filled ice cubes to the punch. Buying generic brands saves you money.

_____

_____

_____

_____

_____

Arranging Details in Order

- The details in a paragraph can be arranged in different ways. One way to arrange details is to put them in the **order** in which they happen.
- Words such as first, next, then, and finally help to show order.

  EXAMPLE: A pineapple-orange ice dessert is easy to make. **First**, combine $\frac{3}{4}$ cup water and $\frac{1}{4}$ cup sugar. **Next**, bring it to a boil, reduce heat, and simmer uncovered for five minutes. **After** cooling slightly, stir in $1\frac{1}{2}$ cups of unsweetened pineapple juice and $\frac{3}{4}$ cup of orange juice. **Then** pour the mixture into a pan. **Finally**, cover the pan with foil and freeze for at least five hours.

- **Write numbers to show the right order in the paragraph.**

_____ It is easy to make tomato cups for salads, such as chicken or tuna. _____ Then cover and chill the tomatoes. _____ Next, use a sharp knife to cut each tomato into sections, without cutting all the way through it. _____ After cutting the tomatoes, spread the sections slightly, and sprinkle a little salt inside. _____ Finally, place spoonfuls of the salad mixture in the middle of each tomato. _____ First, place fresh, ripe tomatoes on a cutting board so that the stems are face down.

> - **Purpose** in writing is the reason why something is written.
> - One purpose is to tell about a thought or feeling.
>   EXAMPLE: I thought I'd never stop laughing.
> - Another purpose is to describe something.
>   EXAMPLE: The bright red color of the bird shone through the waving branches of the trees.
> - Another purpose is to give information.
>   EXAMPLE: The football game is today.
> - Another purpose is to tell about something that is imaginary.
>   EXAMPLE: The snowflakes talked to one another as they fell softly to the ground.

- **Write a sentence that tells how you feel about going to buy a new car.**

_____

- **Write a sentence that describes a new car.**

_____

_____

- **Write a sentence that gives some information about a new car.**

_____

_____

- **Write the first sentence of a story about an imaginary car.**

_____

_____

> Here are some steps to follow in choosing a **topic**.
> - Write a list of persons, things, or animals that interest you. Then circle the topic that especially interests you.
>   EXAMPLES: sports stars, (parties), dogs
> - Divide the topic into smaller parts. Choose the one that you would like to write about.
>   EXAMPLES: decorating for a party, sending out invitations, preparing the food for a party

- **You are going to write a paragraph. Your purpose is to give someone information about how to make something. You need to choose a topic. Write a list of different things you can make.**

1. _____

2. _____

3. _____

4. _____

5. _____

6. _____

- **Circle the topic that especially interests you.**

- **Divide the topic you circled into smaller parts. Underline the one you would like to write about.**

1. _____ 4. _____

2. _____ 5. _____

3. _____ 6. _____

- The purpose of some paragraphs is to give instructions.
- A **how-to paragraph** tells how to do something.
  EXAMPLE:

  How to Make Chocolate Banana Pops

  It is easy to make chocolate banana pops. First, remove the banana peel from the banana. Second, cut the banana into four pieces. Next, push a popsicle stick into the center of each piece. Then put the banana pops on a cookie sheet and freeze them. Carefully melt $\frac{1}{2}$ cup (125 ml) of chocolate chips and 2 tablespoons (30 ml) of margarine in a pan over low heat. Remove the mixture from the heat. Then dip the frozen bananas in the chocolate. Place the chocolate-covered bananas back into the freezer.

- **Write the topic sentence for the paragraph in the box.**

_____

- **Write four sentences that give details about the topic.**

_____

_____

_____

_____

_____

_____

Writing a How-to Paragraph

- **Look at the topic you chose on page 77. Write a how-to paragraph about your topic. Use the model on page 78 to help you. Be sure to include a good topic sentence and the steps you would follow.**

_____

_____

_____

_____

_____

_____

_____

_____

_____

_____

_____

_____

_____

_____

- An **invitation** is a kind of letter. An invitation tells the following things: **who** will give the event, **what** kind of event it will be, **when** it will begin and end, and **where** it will take place.
- An invitation includes the address or telephone number of the sender.

EXAMPLE:

569 North Street
Akron, Ohio 44305
August 6, 2006

Dear Jesse,

   Please come to a dinner party on Saturday, August 19. It will be at Mary Baldwin's house, 22 Oak Avenue, from 6:00 to 9:00. See you then!

Your neighbor,

Call 555-6340   Craig

- **Write an invitation to a party you would like to have.**

_____

_____

_____

_____

_____

_____

_____

_____ _____

- A **telephone message** tells:
  1. The **day** and **time** the message was received.
  2. The **name** of the person getting the message.
  3. The **name** of the person who called.
  4. The **phone number** of the person who called.
  5. The important **information** from the call.
  6. The **name** of the person who took the message.

  EXAMPLE:

  4/18/06

  10:15 A.M.

  Jay–

  Beth Bishop called and wants you to call her back at 555-3958. She needs to ask you how to fix her car.

  Megan

- **Read this part of a telephone call. Then write the message Ming might leave for Gloria. Write today's date and time.**

MING: "Gloria isn't home. I'll take a message for her."

MR. BUTALA: "Please tell her to call me back at 555-2749. I want her to come into work early tomorrow. Thanks. Good-bye."

(Date) _____

(Time) _____

(To) _____

(Message) _____

_____

(From) _____

- **Write each thought as a sentence.**

    1. sewing a shirt

    _____

    2. making a table

    _____

    3. getting a new job

    _____

- **Circle the topic sentence in the paragraph below. Then underline only the sentences that give details about the main idea.**

    A break between acts in a play is needed. It allows time for the crowd to get up and stretch. Stephanie is a very good gardener. It lets the people in the show get ready for the rest of the play. It also gives the audience time to prepare for the next act.

- **Write numbers to show the correct order of the details for each set of directions below.**

    _____ Then let the popcorn pop. _____ First, pour popcorn into a pan. _____ Finally, serve it to the crowd. _____ Next, put a lid on top of the pan.

    _____

    _____ Then mix the juice and water together. _____ Finally, pour the juice into glasses. _____ First, spoon frozen juice into a pitcher. _____ Next, add cold water.

- **Write a sentence that tells how you feel about taking a vacation.**

_____

- **Write a sentence that describes a place you might visit while on vacation.**

_____

_____

- **Write a sentence that gives some information about how to plan a vacation.**

_____

_____

- **Write the first sentence of a story about an imaginary vacation.**

_____

_____

- **Write an invitation to a party you will have after returning from your vacation.**

_____

_____

_____

_____

_____

_____

- **Read this story.**

> One day Sam's car will not start. He has no way to get to work tomorrow. He decides to call his friend Hoan. Hoan lives near Sam. If Hoan can pick him up, Sam will be able to get to work. Sam calls Hoan. Hoan's wife answers the phone. She calls Hoan to the phone. Hoan is able to take Sam to work. He agrees to pick Sam up at 7:30 in the morning. Sam is glad that Hoan can give him a ride.

- **Pretend that Hoan is not home when Sam calls. Write a telephone message for Hoan. Write the important information from the call. Use the correct names, today's date, the time, and your phone number.**

- **Write an invitation to a party you might have at work.**

_____

_____

_____

_____

_____

_____

_____

- **Write a how-to paragraph telling how to get to the place you work. Write a topic sentence and supporting details. Use words such as first, next, and then to put the details in order.**

_____

_____

_____

_____

_____

_____

_____

_____

- **Directions** must be followed step-by-step.
- Sometimes maps help you to follow directions. They might show which way is north, south, east, and west by the letters <u>N</u>, <u>S</u>, <u>E</u>, and <u>W</u>.

EXAMPLE:

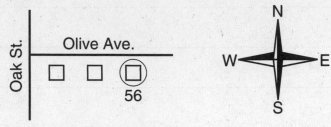

Directions to Mary's House
1) Go north on Oak Street.
2) Turn east on Olive Avenue
3) Walk down 3 houses to 56 Olive Avenue.

- **Look at the map, and read the directions to Joseph's house. Then answer the questions.**

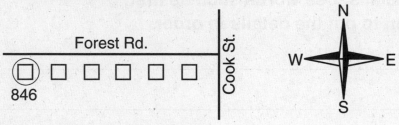

1) Go south on Cook Street.
2) Turn west on Forest Road.
3) Walk down 6 houses to 846 Forest Road.

1. What direction should you go first? _____

2. What street should you walk on first? _____

3. What direction should you go next? _____

4. What street would you be on? _____

5. How many houses down Forest Road is Joseph's house? _____

- Carefully read everything before beginning to follow written directions.
- Pay close attention to words that tell the order of the steps you must follow.   EXAMPLES: first, second, next, later, then, now, finally
- Be sure to follow the directions exactly as they are written.

- **Read the paragraph shown below. Then answer the questions.**

How to Prepare for a Flood

There are many things you can do to prepare for a flood. First, remain calm. Listen to a portable radio for any special instructions for your community. Take valuable items to a location on higher ground. Next, raise heavy things, such as the refrigerator, washer, and dryer, off the ground. Do this by placing concrete blocks, bricks, or stacks of boards under these objects. Before you leave your home, turn off the electricity, gas, and water. Finally, lock your house and go to a safe location.

1. What does this paragraph describe? _____

_____

2. What should you do first? _____

_____

3. Why should you listen to a portable radio? _____

_____

4. What should you use to raise heavy objects off the ground? ___

_____

> ■ Things that are alike in some way can be **grouped** together. The name of the group tells how the things in the group are alike.
>
>   EXAMPLE: Dogs, cats, and horses are all animals.

■ **Underline the words that belong in each group.**

1. **animals**   sand   mouse   monkey   sheep   flower   bird

2. **foods**   bread   hat   egg   carrot   apple   fish

3. **colors**   blue   red   grass   purple   orange   cow

4. **fruits**   apple   cake   orange   milk   banana   grape

5. **clothes**   pants   foot   shirt   jacket   pale   hat

6. **round things**   ball   desk   circle   rake   penny   orange

7. **flying things**   bike   bird   jet   snake   rocket   turtle

8. **men's names**   Peter   Ann   Mike   Jill   Josh   Tom

9. **women's names**   Karen   David   Pam   Bill   Elaine   Melanie

10. **vegetables**   peas   apples   carrots   beans   corn   tuna

11. **tools**   hammer   saw   chair   shovel   rake   desk

■ **Write the words below under the correct heading.**

stove	library	potato
carrot	refrigerator	store
house	corn	toaster

Appliances   **Vegetables**   **Buildings**

_____   _____   _____

_____   _____   _____

_____   _____   _____

■ The **table of contents** is in the front of a book. It lists
titles and page numbers of parts of the book.

EXAMPLE:

Synonyms 5

Antonyms 6

Homonyms 7

More Homonyms 8

Words with More Than One Meaning 9

■ **Use the table of contents in this book to answer
the questions.**

1. How many units are in this book? _____

2. What is the title of Unit 5? _____

3. On what page is "Using Commas in Sentences" in Unit 4? _____

4. What is the title of page 18? _____

5. On what page is "Writing Sentences" in Unit 5? _____

6. What is the title of page 52? _____

7. Which unit would help you learn more about grammar and usage? _____

8. On what page does Unit 6 begin? _____

9. On what page is "Compound Words" in Unit 1? _____

10. On what page does Unit 1 end? _____

11. On what page does the Unit 1 Final Review begin? _____

12. On what page does the Unit 5 Final Review end? _____

> - An **index** is in the back of a book. It lists the subjects of the book in alphabetical order and gives page numbers.
>   EXAMPLE:
>   Abbreviations, 60, 61, 67, 68, 70, 106, 107
>   Adjectives
>   definition of, 47
>   identifying 3, 47, 48, 49, 51, 55, 114
>   that compare, 3, 48, 53, 54, 105, 114
>   that describe, 3, 47, 105, 114

- **Use the index of this book to answer the questions.**

1. On what page is the index of this book? _____

2. What pages tell about suffixes? _____

3. What pages tell about antonyms? _____

4. What pages tell about quotation marks? _____

5. Are the words <u>business letters</u> listed in the index? _____

6. What pages tell about action verbs? _____

7. Under which heading should you look if you want to learn about

   homographs? _____

8. What are three examples of specific punctuation marks that are listed in

   the index? _____

9. Under which heading do you find <u>letter writing</u>? _____

10. What pages tell about telephone messages? _____

11. What pages tell about entry words in a dictionary? _____

12. What pages tell about using commas in letters? _____

> - **Alphabetical order** is the order of the letters in the alphabet. To put words in alphabetical order, look at the first letter of each word. Use the first letter of each word to put the words in the order of the alphabet.
>   EXAMPLES: **b**ag, **p**ack, **c**ottage = **b**ag, **c**ottage, **p**ack
> - Look at the second letter if the words begin with the same letter.
>   EXAMPLES: **fi**sh, **fr**y, **fe**ast = **fe**ast, **fi**sh, **fr**y

- **Write each set of words in alphabetical order.**

oar canoe paddle	giant good glass

1. _____
2. _____
3. _____

1. _____
2. _____
3. _____

town week ranch	bounce ball beach

1. _____
2. _____
3. _____

1. _____
2. _____
3. _____

east soap paddle	pole pump price

1. _____
2. _____
3. _____

1. _____
2. _____
3. _____

- **Guide words** are at the top of each dictionary page. They show the first and last words on the page. Every word listed on the page comes between the guide words.

  EXAMPLE: **oak / real**

oak	⌇⌇⌇⌇⌇
ocean	ready
⌇⌇⌇⌇⌇	real

- **Write the pair of guide words that each word comes between.**

  add / chase   **quack / weep**

  1. beehive ___add / chase___   5. usual _____

  2. reason _____   6. cabin _____

  3. wall _____   7. quiet _____

  4. attach _____   8. spark _____

- **Write the word that would be on the same page with each set of guide words.**

iron	across	ill	dine	dent	job
arrow	weight	ship	wonder	heard	post

  1. idea / in _____   7. cut / desk _____

  2. apple / ax _____   8. serve / space _____

  3. different / dry _____   9. able / ago _____

  4. jar / just _____   10. wheat / wrong _____

  5. insect / island _____   11. hair / hose _____

  6. wagon / winter _____   12. pine / price _____

> - Words that are listed on a dictionary page are called **entry words**. They are listed in alphabetical order.
> - A dictionary gives the **definition**, or meaning, for each entry word.
> - Some words have more than one meaning. Then each meaning is numbered.
>   EXAMPLE:
>   **easy**   **1.** not hard to do.   **2.** free from trouble.

calf 1. a young cow or bull. **2.** the young of other animals.
call 1. to say in a loud voice. **2.** to give a name to. **3.** to make a telephone call.

carol a song.
carpet 1. a floor covering made of heavy cloth. **2.** to cover an area completely.

- **Read the definitions of each entry word. Then answer the questions.**

1. Which word has one meaning? _____

2. Which word has three meanings? _____

3. Which words have two meanings? _____

4. Which word means "a song"? _____

5. Write a sentence with one meaning of carpet. _____

   _____

6. Write a sentence with one meaning of call. _____

   _____

7. Write a sentence with the first meaning of calf. _____

   _____

part **1.** an amount less than the whole. **2.** the line made when hair is combed. **3.** an actor's role.

pass **1.** to go by. **2.** to do the opposite of fail.

peace **1.** freedom from war. **2.** quiet.

pen **1.** something to write with. **2.** a place to keep animals.

place **1.** space taken up by a person or thing. **2.** a city, town, country, or other area. **3.** to put.

plant **1.** a living thing that is not an animal. **2.** to put something in the ground to grow.

point **1.** a sharp end. **2.** a method of scoring a game. **3.** the main idea or important part.

- **The entry words in the box have more than one meaning. Write the number of the correct meaning next to each sentence.**

1. My old red <u>pen</u> ran out of ink. _____

2. Naomi couldn't find a <u>place</u> for her table. _____

3. They will <u>plant</u> daisies in the spring. _____

4. Arnold sat in the chair to get some <u>peace</u>. _____

5. Did most of the people <u>pass</u> the driving test? _____

6. Don't <u>place</u> the candles too near the heat. _____

7. What kind of <u>plant</u> are you growing? _____

8. The pigs were kept in a <u>pen</u>. _____

9. Do you have to travel far to get to the <u>place</u>? _____

10. Did the car <u>pass</u> the truck? _____

11. Do the soldiers want <u>peace</u> or war? _____

12. Kirk scored ten <u>points</u> in the basketball game. _____

13. He only played for <u>part</u> of the game. _____

14. I always try to keep a sharp <u>point</u> on my pencils. _____

15. Everyone had a <u>part</u> in the play. _____

16. There was no <u>part</u> in her hair. _____

- Each word listed in a dictionary is followed by a respelling of the word. The respelling shows how to **pronounce**, or say, the word. The respelling is in parentheses following the entry word.
- **Accent marks** show which word parts are said with the most force.   EXAMPLES: sər prīz′   tē′ chər
- A **pronunciation key** (shown below) contains letters and special symbols, along with sample words, that show how the letters should be pronounced.

- **Use the pronunciation key to answer the following questions.**

  at; āpe; fär; câre; end; mē; it; īce; pîerce; hot; ōld, sông; fôrk; oil; out; up; ūse; rüle; pùll; tûrn; chin; sing; shop; thin; <u>th</u>is; hw in white; zh in treasure. The symbol ə stands for the unstressed vowel sound in about, taken, pencil, lemon, and circus.

  1. What key word is given for ù? _____

  2. What key word is given for î? _____

  3. What key words are given for ə? _____

- **Study each respelling using the pronunciation key. Then circle the word that matches the respelling.**

  1. (chōz)   shoes   chose   choice

  2. (let′ ûr)   letter   lettuce   ladder

  3. (sī′ əns)   since   scenes   science

  4. (kär′ tən)   cartoon   carton   garden

  5. (<u>th</u>ēz) these   this   those

  6. (mezh′ ûr)   messier   messenger   measure

  7. (fü′ əl)   fuel   full   file

  8. (thim′ bəl)   symbol   thimble   tumble

  9. (loi′ əl)   loyal   local   low

  10. (shûr)   shore   sir   sure

■ **Read the directions below. Then answer the questions.**

You can easily put a smoke detector in your home. First, decide where you want to put the detector. Second, use screws to attach the detector's bracket to the wall. Next, put a battery into the bracket. Then attach the detector to the bracket by twisting or snapping it into place. Finally, be sure to test your smoke detector at least once a month.

1. What can you do using these directions? _____

2. What should you do first? _____

3. What should you do after you attach the detector's bracket to the wall?

_____

4. How should you attach the detector to the bracket? _____

_____

5. How often should you test your detector? _____

■ **Circle the words that belong in each group.**

1. **months**   May   March   John   July   April   Friday

2. **seasons**   fall   day   spring   summer   rain   winter

3. **fruit**   beans   apples   oranges   peas   pears   seeds

■ **Write the name of the group for each set of words.**

1. pants   dress   shirt   skirt   coat   _____

2. lunch   supper   breakfast   dinner   _____

3. red   green   yellow   blue   orange   _____

- **Write each list of words in alphabetical order.**

  1. seen _____   **2.** blue _____   **3.** press _____

       lake _____   bee _____   plow _____

       cage _____   bat _____   puff _____

- **Use the index in this book to answer the following questions.**

  1. What page gives a definition of adverbs? _____

  2. What pages tell about exclamation points? _____

  3. What pages tell about homonyms? _____

- **Read the dictionary entries for <u>stalk</u> and <u>stand</u>. Write the meaning that goes with each sentence below.**

  > **stalk 1.** the stem of a plant. **2.** to hunt.
  > **stand 1.** to be on one's feet. **2.** to put up with.

  1. I watched the cat stalk the wind-up toy.

  _____

  2. Let's stand up and stretch.

  _____

  3. We put the stalk in water to keep the plant alive.

  _____

  4. I can't stand the smell of onions.

  _____

- **Study each respelling using the pronunciation key. Then circle the word that matches the respelling.**

  1. (ô′ fùl)   official   awful   useful

  2. (rīm)   rhyme   rim   room

  3. (van)   vane   van   than

  4. (our)   are   or   hour

  5. (weth′ ər)   weather   wither   whisper

  > at; āpe; fär; câre; end; mē; it; īce; pîerce; hot; ōld, sông; fôrk; oil; out; up; ūse; rüle; pùll; tûrn; chin; sing; shop; thin; this; hw in white; zh in treasure. The symbol ə stands for the unstressed vowel sound in about, taken, pencil, lemon, and circus.

- Imagine you are going shopping in a grocery store. To make your shopping trip quicker and easier, put the food items on the shopping list below into the groups in which they belong.

Shopping List: canned soup, potatoes, bananas, frozen orange juice, lettuce, chicken, broccoli, hamburger, apples, bacon

Fruits	Canned	Vegetables
_____	_____	_____
_____	_____	_____
_____	_____	_____

Frozen	Meat
_____	_____
_____	_____
_____	_____

- Use the table of contents in this book to answer the following questions.

1. What is the title of page 29?_____

2. On what page is "Linking Verbs" in Unit 3?_____

3. On what page is "Guide Words" in Unit 6?_____

4. What is the title of page 89?_____

5. How many pages are in Unit 1?_____

6. What is the title of Unit 2?_____

- **Follow the directions to Diane's house. Circle her house on the map.**

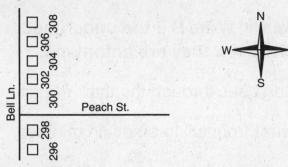

1. Go west on Peach Street.
2. Turn north on Bell Lane.
3. Go down 5 houses to 308 Bell Lane.

- **Write directions to 296 Bell Lane.**

_____

_____

- **Draw a map showing the street where you live. Draw a line to show what street crosses yours. Then write directions to where you live.**

_____

_____

Synonyms and Antonyms ▪ Write S if the underlined words are synonyms. Write A if they are antonyms.

_____ 1. The driver couldn't see through the thick fog and mist.

_____ 2. The gas tank went from full to empty in minutes.

_____ 3. We couldn't see to our right or to our left.

_____ 4. We had to stop on the side and wait for help because our car just wouldn't go anymore.

_____ 5. We stopped when it was light outside, but now it is getting dark.

_____ 6. We thought it would be a short wait, but no one came for a long time.

_____ 7. We tried to push and shove the car.

_____ 8. A man gave us some gas and said we would be wise to go to a gas station, since we were foolish enough to run out of gas.

_____ 9. We stopped at a gas station, and then started our trip home.

_____10. We were so happy to be home that we forgot how sad we had been.

Homonyms ▪ Circle the correct homonym to complete each sentence.

1. Shanelle has been invited (two, to, too) a movie.

2. Denise is going to the movie, (too, to, two).

3. Shanelle did not (here, hear) what time the movie begins.

4. She asks Denise if the movie starts at (to, too, two) o'clock.

5. Denise tells Shanelle that she needs to be (there, their, they're) at four o'clock.

6. They plan to meet (here, hear) and go together.

7. (Their, They're, There) going to have a good time.

Words with More Than One Meaning ▪ Read the meanings in the box. Write the number of the meaning for each underlined word.

> **pound 1.** a weight equal to 16 ounces **2.** to hit hard over and over
> **light 1.** not heavy **2.** something by which we see

1. Tony turned on the <u>light</u> so he could see. _____

2. He picked up a <u>light</u> piece of wood. _____

3. It weighed less than one <u>pound</u>. _____

4. He used a tool to <u>pound</u> a design into the wood. _____

Prefixes ▪ Underline the prefix. Write the meaning of the word.

1. unable _____

2. relive _____

3. repay _____

4. untrue _____

Suffixes ▪ Underline the suffix. Write the meaning of the word.

1. worker _____

2. dryer _____

3. visitor _____

4. marker _____

Compound Words and Contractions ▪ Make a compound word or a contraction from each pair of words. Circle the contractions.

1. some + one = _____

2. he + is = _____

3. I + will = _____

4. day + light = _____

Types of Sentences ▪ Write <u>S</u> for <u>statement</u>, <u>Q</u> for <u>question</u>, <u>C</u> for <u>command</u>, or <u>E</u> for <u>exclamation</u> for each sentence. Write <u>X</u> if the group of words is not a sentence.

_____ 1. Rob played basketball.

_____ 2. How many points did Lee score?

_____ 3. What a good player she is!

_____ 4. Pass the ball to Lupe.

_____ 5. Scored ten points.

_____ 6. Which team do you think will win?

_____ 7. I hope that Pat's team wins.

_____ 8. Both teams are doing a.

_____ 9. Lupe bounced the ball to Rob.

_____ 10. Shoot the ball, Rob.

Subjects and Predicates ▪ Underline each subject. Circle each predicate.

1. Mr. and Mrs. Fleming took care of their grandchildren on Saturday.
2. Mr. Fleming bought a pizza for lunch.
3. Mrs. Fleming played games with the children.
4. Mr. Fleming read a book to the children.
5. The book was about a knight.
6. The children asked if they could watch cartoons.
7. Mrs. Fleming turned on some cartoons.
8. Everyone laughed at the silly cartoons.
9. Mr. and Mrs. Fleming baked cookies for the children.
10. It was time for the children to go home.

Combining Subjects and Predicates ▪ Combine the sentences. Write the new sentences.

1. Dan car-pooled with Alex. Dan worked with Alex.

_____

2. Vicenté wanted to apply for a new job. Tammy wanted to apply for a new job.

_____

3. They worked today. They were off last Monday.

_____

4. Vicenté works inside the plant. Tammy works outside the plant.

_____

5. You can apply for the new job. You can continue working at your current job.

_____

Writing Clear Sentences ▪ Read the sentences. Write two sentences for each.

1. Mark enjoys all kinds of sports, his favorite sport is soccer.

_____

_____

2. Mark's wife used to play soccer, she was on a team in high school.

_____

_____

3. Mark finds a photo of his wife playing soccer, he shows it to his friend Jamal.

_____

_____

4. Jamal's wife is in the photo, his wife used to play soccer, too.

_____

_____

Singular and Plural Nouns ▪ Write <u>S</u> before each
singular noun. Then write its plural form. Write <u>P</u>
before each plural noun. Then write its singular form.

_____ 1. inches _____   _____ 4. boxes _____

_____ 2. toe _____   _____ 5. cart _____

_____ 3. bus _____   _____ 6. wrenches _____

Proper and Common Nouns ▪ Write <u>P</u> before
each proper noun. Then write a common noun for
it. Write <u>C</u> before each common noun. Then write
a proper noun for it.

_____ 1. friend _____   _____ 3. school _____

_____ 2. Texas _____   _____ 4. Lake Erie _____

Verbs ▪ Underline each action verb. Circle each
linking verb. Write <u>present</u> or <u>past</u>.

1. Kate lives in Chicago. _____

2. I visited her in June. _____

3. Diane was in Chicago last year. _____

Using the Correct Verb ▪ Draw a line under the
correct verb.

1. Joel (saw, seen) the train pulling out of the station.

2. He needed to (buy, buys) a ticket to Chicago, Illinois.

3. Joel (runs, run) to catch the train.

4. He should (have, has) gotten there earlier.

5. Joel (were, was) waving to get the train to stop.

6. But the train (did, do) not stop.

Using the Correct Pronoun ▪ Draw a line under the correct pronoun.

1. Kamal's wife gave (him, he) a new camera.
2. He wants to learn how to take pictures with (them, it).
3. (He, His) wife will show him how the camera works.
4. First, (them, they) must find something to photograph.
5. Kamal finds their little boy asleep in (he, his) room.
6. He thinks (him, he) looks cute.
7. He decides (they, their) should take a picture of him.
8. Kamal and (he, his) wife take the picture.
9. Rajiv and (I, me) are Kamal's brothers.
10. We hope he sends (we, us) a copy of our nephew's photo.

Adjectives ▪ Underline each adjective.

1. Dinosaurs were once the largest reptiles on Earth.
2. Some dinosaurs ate green plants.
3. Other animals felt safer around dinosaurs that ate plants.
4. Some dinosaurs ate fresh meat.
5. It was dangerous for other animals to be close to one of these hungry dinosaurs.

Adverbs ▪ Underline each adverb.

1. Many kinds of dinosaurs lived together.
2. Scientists have carefully studied how dinosaurs lived.
3. There are no dinosaurs alive today.
4. Scientists do not know exactly what happened to them, since it was so long ago.
5. They have worked very hard to find reasons why the dinosaurs died.

Capitalizing Proper Nouns ▪ Rewrite the words.
Use capital letters where needed.

1. december _____

2. winter _____

3. monday _____

4. my daughter _____

5. louise _____

6. new year's day _____

7. california _____

8. denver _____

9. thanksgiving _____

10. canada _____

11. tomás _____

12. store _____

Capitalization ▪ Circle the letters that should be capitalized.

1. my family and I live in orlando, florida.

2. we moved here from huntsville, texas, last summer.

3. i work in a museum.

4. it is called the charles c. adler museum.

5. the museum is north of my home.

6. it is on jones street near academy theater.

7. the museum is closed on sundays and mondays.

8. ms. n. kelly is my boss.

9. ms. kelly is getting the museum ready for a large dinosaur display.

10. the display will be set up on the first tuesday in march.

11. i'm going to help make sure the display is perfect.

12. students from oak springs elementary will be the first to view our dinosaurs.

Punctuation ▪ Put periods, commas, question marks, quotation marks, and apostrophes where needed.

1. Ms N Kelly asked Are you ready to set up the dinosaur display

2. Yes I was ready for the dinosaurs to arrive

3. The workers brought in dinosaur bones footprints and models

4. I didnt count all the boxes, but I could tell that this dinosaur display was going to be huge

5. One worker said I cant get this model through the door

6. Youll have to take it in through the back I said

7. I worked on Wednesday Thursday and Friday setting up the display

8. I asked my boss if she liked the display

9. Ms Kelly said Yes I am very pleased with the job you have done

10. Id bet the children cant wait to see the dinosaurs I said

Parts of a Letter ▪ Rewrite these parts of a letter. Use capital letters and commas where they are needed.

1. dear zach _____

2. june 1 2006 _____

3. houston texas 77072 _____

4. sincerely _____

5. april 9 2006 _____

6. your friend _____

7. dear jesse _____

8. kansas city missouri 64114 _____

Writing Sentences ▪ Write each thought as a sentence.

1. watching television after dinner

_____

2. laughing at the funny lines

_____

3. eating popcorn as I watch

_____

Writing Paragraphs ▪ Circle the topic sentence in each paragraph. Then number the sentences in the correct order.

_____ Next, practice saying your speech in front of

a mirror. _____ The first thing you can do to make

yourself feel better is to get used to being on a stage.

_____ Finally, ask some friends or family members if they

will listen to you practice. _____ Most people get scared

when they have to give a speech.

_____

_____ First, she pulled all of the weeds in her garden.

_____ Yesterday Ms. Yamata worked in her garden.

_____ When Ms. Yamata was finished, she drank a large

glass of lemonade. _____ Then she planted some tulips,

daisies, and roses.

Writing a How-to Paragraph ▪ Write a paragraph that tells how to make your favorite recipe. Be sure to include a good topic sentence and the steps you would follow.

_____

_____

_____

_____

_____

_____

Writing a Telephone Message ▪ Read this part of a telephone call. Then write the message Claudia might leave for Tony. Write today's date and time.

CLAUDIA: "No, I'm sorry. Tony isn't home right now. May I take a message?"

KIM: "Yes, please tell him that he needs to call me at work. The number here is 555-9487. I need to ask him about a computer problem we are having. Thank you. Good-bye."

(Date) _____

(Time) _____

(To) _____

(Message) _____

_____

(From) _____

Following Written Directions ▪ **Read the directions, and study the map. Then answer the questions.**

Go east past the high school. Turn north on Oak Road. Go three blocks until Oak Road ends.

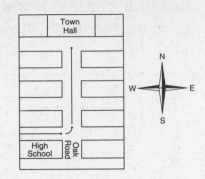

1. Which direction do you go to pass the high school? _____

2. What is the name of the road on which you turn north? _____

3. To what building do these directions lead you? _____

Grouping ▪ **Write the words below under the correct heading.**

| toast | spaghetti | pancakes |
| fish | popcorn | raisins |

Breakfast   **Dinner**   **Snacks**

_____   _____   _____

_____   _____   _____

Using a Table of Contents and an Index ▪ **Answer the following questions.**

1. Where in a book would you find a table of contents? _____

2. What information does a table of contents list? _____

3. Where in a book would you find an index? _____

4. In what order are the subjects listed in an index? _____

Alphabetical Order ▪ Write each list of words in alphabetical order.

1. rake _____
   scare _____
   sat _____

2. teeth _____
   cause _____
   cheer _____

Guide Words ▪ Study the dictionary page on the right. Write the guide words for the page.

leather ᴜᴜᴜ ᴜᴜᴜᴜᴜ ᴜᴜᴜ
ᴜᴜᴜ ᴜᴜᴜᴜᴜ   ᴜᴜ ᴜᴜ ᴜᴜ
ᴜᴜᴜ ᴜᴜᴜᴜ ᴜᴜᴜ ᴜᴜ ᴜᴜ
ᴜᴜᴜ ᴜᴜᴜ   ᴜᴜᴜᴜᴜᴜ
ᴜᴜᴜᴜᴜᴜᴜᴜ lie ᴜᴜᴜᴜ

_____ / _____

Words with More Than One Meaning ▪ Read the dictionary entry for <u>batter</u>. Write the number of the meaning that is used in each sentence.

_____ 1. James mixed the <u>batter</u> for two minutes.

_____ 2. The second <u>batter</u> hit a home run.

batter 1. a mixture of flour, milk, and eggs used in cooking. **2.** a player whose turn it is to bat.

Pronunciation ▪ Study each respelling using the pronunciation key. Then circle the word that matches the respelling.

1. (noi′ zē)   nose   notes   noisy

2. (drô′ ing)   growing   drawing   drowning

3. (sum′ ər)   summary   summer   simmer

4. (fus)   fuse   fuss   fish

5. (ə wâr′)   beware   aware   wear

6. (on′ ûr)   under   onward   honor

at; āpe; fär; câre; end; mē; it; īce; pîerce; hot; ōld, sông; fôrk; oil; out; up; ūse; rüle; pull; tûrn; chin; sing; shop; thin; <u>th</u>is; **hw** in white; **zh** in treasure. The symbol ə stands for the unstressed vowel sound in about, taken, pencil, lemon, and circus.

A. Write <u>S</u> before each pair of synonyms, <u>A</u> before each pair of antonyms, and <u>H</u> before each pair of homonyms.

_____ **1.** hear, here   _____ **3.** road, rode

_____ **2.** big, large   _____ **4.** start, finish

B. Read the meanings. Write the number of the meaning of each underlined word.

_____ **1.** The driver made a <u>sharp</u> left turn.

_____ **2.** Jeff met Susan at four o'clock <u>sharp</u>.

> **sharp** **1.** having a point or edge that can cut. **2.** to turn in a sudden way. **3.** to be somewhere at an exact time.

C. Write <u>P</u> before each word with a prefix, <u>S</u> before each word with a suffix, and <u>C</u> before each compound word.

_____ **1.** untie   _____ **3.** visitor

_____ **2.** sunshine   _____ **4.** rainbow

D. Write the words that make up each contraction.

1. I'm _____ _____   **3.** he's _____ _____

2. she'll _____ _____   **4.** can't _____ _____

E. Write <u>S</u> before the statement, <u>Q</u> before the question, <u>C</u> before the command, and <u>E</u> before the exclamation. Then underline the subject, and circle the predicate in each sentence.

_____ **1.** Where are you going?   _____ **3.** Pack plenty of sunscreen.

_____ **2.** I am going to Mexico.   _____ **4.** I can't wait until next week!

F. Combine the sentences. Write the new sentence.

1. Jane had an appointment. Andy had an appointment.

_____

2. Jessie lives in north Glenview. Jessie works in south Glenview.

_____

G. Read the sentences. Write two sentences for each.

1. I went to an interview, I hope I get the job.

_____

_____

2. Candace has a date, she's going to a movie.

_____

_____

H. Write S before each singular noun and P before each plural noun. Then circle the common nouns, and underline the proper nouns.

_____ 1. book   _____ 3. chairs

_____ 2. Fridays   _____ 4. California

I. Write A if the underlined verb is an action verb, L if it is a linking verb, or H if it is a helping verb.

_____ 1. Many people in line are angry.

_____ 2. Some of them will not wait much longer.

_____ 3. One person asked why the line is moving so slowly.

J. Write past or present on the lines.

_____ 1. Randy drives to the store.

_____ 2. He bought some groceries yesterday.

K. Circle the correct pronoun in each sentence.

1. Some of (me, my) friends are coming over.

2. (They, Them) will be here after dinner.

3. I will make (they, them) some dessert.

L. On the line before each sentence, write adjective or adverb to describe the underlined word.

_____ 1. Felipé slowly told the joke.

_____ 2. It was the funniest joke I've ever heard.

M. In the letter below, underline the letters that should be capitalized, and add punctuation where needed.

8406 canton rd

rawlins wyoming 82301

apr 12 2006

dear ms burke

ive been living in your apartment complex for three

years_____ some people ask doesnt ms burke care about her

apartments_____ yes i think you do_____ i say i think ms

burkes apartments are great_____ maybe you could fix the

plumbing wallpaper and carpeting_____ then people would

be happier_____

sincerely

pat janson

N. Write a topic sentence and two sentences with supporting details on the topic of health care.

_____

_____

O. Number the following directions in order.

_____ **1.** Finally, stop at the second house on the right.

_____ **2.** Then go two miles.

_____ **3.** First, turn west on Willow Drive.

P. Write the words in alphabetical order.

1. honest _____

2. hour _____

3. handle _____

4. hope _____

Q. Use the dictionary entries to answer the questions.

1. Which words have two meanings?_____

2. Which word has three meanings? _____

3. Which word means "freedom from war"? _____

> **pass 1.** to go by. **2.** to do the opposite of fail.
> **peace 1.** freedom from war. **2.** quiet
> **place 1.** space taken up by a person or thing. **2.** a city, town, country or other area. **3.** to put.

Below is a list of the sections on *Check What You've Learned* and the pages on which the skills in each section are taught. If you missed any questions, turn to the pages listed, and practice the skills. Then correct the problems you missed on *Check What You've Learned*.

Section	Practice Page	Section	Practice Page	Section	Practice Page
Unit 1		F	24–25	*Unit 4*	
A	5–8	G	26	M	56–66
B	9	*Unit 3*		*Unit 5*	
C	10–12	H	31–33	N	72–75
D	13	I	34–42	*Unit 6*	
		J	35, 36	O	75, 86, 87
Unit 2		K	43–46	P	91
E	20–23	L	47–51	Q	93, 94

Check What You Know (P. 1)

A. 1. A
2. H
3. A
4. S

B. 1. 1
2. 3

C. 1. C
2. S
3. P
4. P

D. 1. is not
2. I will
3. you are
4. that is

The words in bold should be circled.

E. 1. E <u>That</u> **is an amazing sight**!
2. Q **What do** <u>you</u> **think that thing is**?
3. S <u>It</u> **looks like some kind of spaceship**.
4. C <u>(You)</u> **Protect your eyes from the bright lights**.

Check What You Know (P. 2)

F. 1. The weather is hot and humid.
2. The sun might shine, or it might rain.

G. 1. Osato has a vegetable garden. She waters it every day.
2. Gary bakes bread. He uses it when he makes sandwiches.

The words in bold should be circled.

H. 1. P **taxes**
2. S <u>Eduardo</u>
3. S **computer**
4. P <u>Andes Mountains</u>

I. 1. A
2. L
3. H

J. 1. present
2. past

Check What You Know (P. 3)

K. 1. I
2. He
3. him

L. 1. adjective
2. adverb

M.
1748 <u>E</u>. First <u>St</u>.
Kansas <u>City</u>, <u>Missouri</u> 64114
Jan. 12, 2006

Dear <u>Mr</u>. Haas,
Thank you for setting up an interview with me for next <u>Tuesday</u>. Yes, I've done well here working on televisions, radios, and dvd players. <u>Did</u> you know that I'm learning how to work on computers? It is easier than I thought. I fixed my friend's computer last week. I'll tell you more about this on <u>Tuesday</u>.
Sincerely,
<u>William</u> <u>Thurston</u>

N. Discuss your answers with your instructor.

Check What You Know (P. 4)

O. 1. 2
2. 3
3. 1

P. 1. manage
2. mention
3. money
4. mystery

Q. **1.** shave
2. sharp
3. shed

 Vocabulary

Lesson 1, Synonyms (P. 5)

Top:

I sat down to eat my <u>supper</u>. Suddenly, I heard an <u>odd</u> noise. The noise came from <u>beneath</u> the kitchen sink. I was worried that I had a <u>large</u> crack in the pipe. But I saw that it was just a <u>tiny</u> leak. I <u>started</u> to work on the leak. It did not take long to <u>repair</u> the pipe. I was <u>done</u> in just a few minutes.

Bottom:
Discuss your answer with your instructor.

Lesson 2, Antonyms (P. 6)

Top:

It is <u>easy</u> to use a checkbook. I write checks for the things I <u>buy</u>. I make sure I sign my name at the <u>bottom</u> of the check. I <u>give</u> the check to the store clerk. Then I <u>subtract</u> the amount of the check from my balance.

Bottom:
1. Do you think Ann will win or lose?
2. Will he return to work now or later?

Lesson 3, Homonyms (P. 7)

Top:
1. their
2. there
3. they're
4. their
5. there
6. they're
7. their

Bottom:
Discuss your answer with your instructor.

Lesson 4, More Homonyms (P. 8)

1. to
2. to
3. hear
4. too
5. to
6. two
7. there
8. two
9. too
10. to
11. here
12. to

Lesson 5, Words with More Than One Meaning (P. 9)

Top:
1. 2
2. 2
3. 2
4. 1
5. 1
6. 1
7. 1
8. 2

Bottom:
Discuss your answer with your instructor.

Lesson 6, Prefixes (P. 10)

Top:
1. unhappy, not happy
2. unfair, not fair
3. uneven, not even
4. unsafe, not safe
5. unfit, not fit

Middle:
1. reopen, open again
2. retest, test again
3. reuse, use again
4. reread, read again

Bottom:
Discuss your answers with your instructor.

Lesson 7, Suffixes (P. 11)

Top:
1. climber
2. teacher
3. visitor
4. traveler
5. actor
6. marker
7. painter
8. singer

Bottom:
1. The <u>gardener</u> clipped the roses.
2. He cleaned his gloves in the <u>washer</u>.
3. He and a <u>farmer</u> ate lunch.
4. Then he hired a new <u>worker</u> to help him.
5. His new helper used to be a <u>teacher</u>.

Lesson 8, Compound Words (P. 12)

Top:
1. birthday
2. afternoon
3. farmhouse
4. fireplace
5. catfish
6. rainbow
7. thunderstorm
8. sunrise
9. waterfall
10. downstairs

Bottom:
1. birth   day
2. every   one
3. in   side
4. Every   thing
5. door   bell
6. No   body
7. Some   body

Lesson 9, Contractions (P. 13)

Top:
1. She's going camping this weekend.
2. I think she'll go fishing in the lake.
3. Inuk doesn't like to fish.
4. Here's some fresh bait.
5. There's enough for everyone to use.
6. After we catch the fish, I'll help cook them.
7. It isn't hard to do.

Bottom:
Discuss your answer with your instructor.

Review (P. 14)

Top:
1. home
2. market
3. sack
4. big
5. nice

Middle:
1. open
2. early
3. rainy
4. run
5. stop

Bottom:
1. two
2. here
3. too
4. to
5. there
6. they're
7. too

Review (P. 15)

Discuss your answer with your instructor.

Discuss your answer with your instructor.

1. unpack
2. recopy
3. untie
4. relive
5. remake
6. retake
7. rename
8. untrue
9. unsure

1. cleaner
2. visitor
3. worker
4. teacher
5. dryer
6. actor
7. heater
8. leader
9. sailor

The words in bold should be circled.
1. I'd like a **weekend** job.
2. Isn't there one in the **newspaper**?
3. Yes, here's **something**.
4. There's a job with the **railroad**.
5. I can't go **today**.
6. I'll go Monday **afternoon**.

Using What You've Learned (P. 16)

Dear Mr. Jones,
  Please tell your workers they're making too much noise. I hear them early in the morning. They're always waking me up, and I can't go back to sleep. I shouldn't have to listen to their noise. I don't think they should start working here until 8 o'clock. I'm sure we can find a way to solve this problem.

Using What You've Learned (P. 17)

Discuss your answer with your instructor.

 Unit 2 Sentences

Lesson 10, Sentences (P. 18)

Top:
1, 3, 5, and 7 are sentences.
Bottom:
1. The ants marched in a row.
2. They were looking for crumbs.
3. Rosa saw them coming.
4. She moved their blanket right away.
5. The food was for Daniel, not the ants.

Lesson 11, Identifying Sentences (P. 19)

Top:
1. Katarina read about a car show.
2. She went to the car show.
3. Some cars were for the future.
4. How many cars were there?
5. Katarina liked an old car best.
6. Did it win a blue ribbon?
7. Yes, it won "Best of Show."

Bottom:
The following should be crossed out:
Looked at different types of cars.
Several judges looked at.
Felt it should win.

Lesson 12, Statements and Questions (P. 20)

Top:
1. S	6. S
2. Q	7. S
3. S	8. S
4. S	9. Q
5. Q	10. Q

Bottom:
  Many people visit Hawaii to ride the waves. Which beach do they like best?

Lesson 13, Commands and Exclamations (P. 21)

Top:
1. E
2. C
3. C
4. E
5. C
6. E
7. C
8. E
9. E

Bottom:
Discuss your answers with your instructor.

Lesson 14, Subjects in Sentences (P. 22)

Top:
1. We went skiing today.
2. The snow was just right.
3. I flew down the hill.
4. Kamal lost his hat.
5. The hat was buried in the snow.
6. Skaters were on the pond.
7. The ice was smooth.
8. My son liked ice skating the best.
9. He skated very fast.
10. Our family watched him.

Bottom:
Discuss your answers with your instructor.

Lesson 15, Predicates in Sentences (P. 23)

Top:
1. John took his children to the zoo.
2. The lion cub growled at a bird.
3. The huge ape swung from a bar.
4. Barry liked the camels.
5. These tiny snakes are harmless.
6. Monkeys are fun to watch.
7. Vince fed an elephant.
8. Two elephants were in the pen.
9. Barbara saw the baby alligators.
10. They walked all around the zoo.

Bottom:
Discuss your answers with your instructor.

Lesson 16, Combining Subjects and Predicates (P. 24)

1. Charlene and the children got on the bus.
2. Bill and his brother stood in line for the tickets.
3. Bill said good-bye to his brother and picked up his suitcase.
4. He got on the bus and sat next to Charlene.
5. Charlene read a book and played with the children.
6. Bill ate lunch and wrote a letter.
7. The bus moved quickly and arrived on time.

Lesson 17, Combining Sentences (P. 25)

Top:
1. The wind howled, and the sand blew around.
2. The people can swim, or they can sit on the beach.
3. The water is cold, but the sand is warm.
4. The sea is blue, and the foam is white.
5. Rick carried our lunch, and we carried the chairs.

Bottom:
1. Take your towel, and lay it on the beach.
2. You can walk in the sand, or you can wade in the water.
3. We can't use glass bottles on the beach, but we can use plastic bottles.

Lesson 18, Writing Clear Sentences (P. 26)

1. The seeds must be planted.
   This is done in many ways.
2. A seed floated in the breeze.
   It was very windy.
3. You can eat these seeds.
   Shameka will gather some more.
4. Birds and animals eat seeds.
   You can buy seeds for them in a store.

Review (P. 27)

1. Owls have large eyes.
2. They live in the ocean.
3. Lizards are reptiles.
4. Do you like chipmunks?

1. Q
2. S
3. Q
4. S

1. C
2. E
3. C
4. E

The words in bold should be circled.
1. The <u>cat</u> **washed its face with its paw**.
2. <u>Kirk</u> **threw a ball of yarn to the cat**.
3. The <u>cat</u> **took a long nap**.
4. <u>Kirk</u> **fed the cat after its nap**.

Review (P. 28)

Top:
1. Erin fed the baby and put her in bed.
2. Raul and Erin cleaned the house.
3. Their friends were early, but Raul and Erin were ready to greet them.

Bottom:
1. My friend comes over.
   We go to see a movie.
2. We stand in line.
   We get our tickets.
3. We find a place to sit.
   We share some popcorn.
4. The theater gets dark.
   The movie begins.

Using What You've Learned (P. 29)

Keiko is moving into a new apartment. It is much bigger than her old one, and it is only a few miles away from her job. She has already moved most of her things, but she cannot move her furniture. She has hired a moving company to take her furniture, and the movers will be there at noon. She is excited about moving.

Using What You've Learned (P. 30)

Discuss your answers with your instructor.

 Unit 3 Grammar and Usage

Lesson 19, Nouns (P. 31)

Top:
1. The <u>astronaut</u> looked out the <u>window</u>.
2. <u>Clouds</u> circled the <u>earth</u>.
3. The <u>ocean</u> looked like a <u>lake</u>.
4. Another <u>astronaut</u> ate her <u>lunch</u>.
5. An <u>apple</u> floated inside the <u>cabin</u>.
6. One <u>man</u> put on his <u>spacesuit</u>.
7. The <u>astronaut</u> walked in <u>space</u>.
8. The <u>newspaper</u> had <u>pictures</u> of him.

Bottom:
1. ocean
2. ship
3. doctor
4. radio
5. cheer
6. day

Lesson 20, Singular and Plural Nouns (P. 32)

Top:
1. skates
2. cars
3. parades
4. toes
5. brushes
6. classes
7. inches
8. boxes
9. dishes
10. dollars
11. leashes
12. watches

Bottom:
1. The fish are in a new tank.
2. All the plants are fresh.
3. The fish are hiding in those castles.
4. Use that net to catch the fish.

Lesson 21, Common and Proper Nouns (P. 33)

Top:
1. C	7. C
2. P	8. P
3. C	9. P
4. C	10. P
5. P	11. C
6. P	12. C

Bottom:
The words in bold should be circled.
1. The <u>ocean</u> was very rough on **Tuesday**.
2. The <u>waves</u> pounded **Sand Beach**.
3. The <u>beach</u> is in **Mexico**.
4. Some <u>people</u> were there from **Portland**.
5. **Julio** spied a <u>seaplane</u>.
6. Another <u>man</u> saw a **Flying Eagle**.
7. The <u>plane</u> was flying to **Canada**.
8. **Sarah** waved to the <u>pilot</u>.

Lesson 22, Action Verbs (P. 34)

Top:
1. took
2. flew
3. chattered
4. drank
5. leaped

Middle:
1. roar
2. grow
3. swing
4. buzz
5. search

Bottom:
Discuss your answer with your instructor.

Lesson 23, Verbs in the Present (P. 35)

Top:
1. moves
2. lives
3. help
4. tells
5. learns
6. invite
7. talk
8. enjoys

Bottom:
Discuss your answers with your instructor.

Lesson 24, Verbs in the Past (P. 36)

Top:
1. like
2. P turned
3. P stopped
4. P waited
5. jog
6. P rested

Bottom:
1. My friends and I entered the five-mile race.
2. We started the race together.
3. We walked up a steep hill.
4. I hoped to win.
5. I finished in first place.

Lesson 25, Linking Verbs (P. 37)

Top:
1. L
4. L
6. L
9. L
11. L

Bottom:
Discuss your answer with your instructor.

Lesson 26, Using *Am, Is,* and *Are* (P. 38)

Line 1. are; is
Line 3. is
Line 4. is
Line 5. are; is
Line 7. am
Line 9. is
Line 10. am
Line 12. are
Line 13. are

Lesson 27, Using *Was* and *Were* (P. 39)

1. was
2. was
3. were
4. was
5. was
6. was
7. were
8. were
9. was
10. were
11. was
12. were
13. were
14. was
15. were

Lesson 28, Helping Verbs (P. 40)

Top:
The words in bold should be circled.
1. The sun has **risen**.
2. The roosters had **remembered** to crow.
3. The cows have **chewed** the grass.
4. Rita had **collected** the eggs.
5. Ben has **baked** some fresh bread.
6. We have **eaten** breakfast.

Bottom:
1. I have walked to the park.
2. A gentle rain has started.
3. It had rained yesterday.
4. Pat had bought an umbrella last week.

Lesson 29, Using Forms of *Do* and *See* (P. 41)

Top:
1. Do
2. do
3. does

Bottom:
1. seen
2. see
3. saw

Lesson 30, Using Forms of *Give* and *Go* (P. 42)

Top:
1. gave
2. given
3. gives
4. given

Bottom:
1. go
2. goes
3. gone
4. goes
5. go
6. went
7. go
8. gone

Lesson 31, Pronouns (P. 43)

Top:
1. Maria invited them over to watch a movie.
2. She made popcorn for her friends.
3. Hot air tosses it around.
4. He put salt on his popcorn.
5. Don gave some popcorn to her.
6. Sue passed the bowl to them.

Bottom:
Discuss your answers with your instructor.

Lesson 32, Subject and Object Pronouns (P. 44)

Top:
1. O   4. O
2. S   5. S
3. S   6. S

Bottom:
1. We went to the rodeo.
2. One woman roped them.
3. He couldn't believe her strength.
4. The woman gave us a smile when she won.

Lesson 33, Possessive Pronouns (P. 45)

Top:
1. their   4. her
2. Their   5. his
3. Our   6. our

Bottom:
1. His
2. My
3. Her
4. Their
5. Our
6. Your
7. Its
8. His

Lesson 34, Using *I* or *Me* (P. 46)

1. Karen; I
2. her; me
3. Karen; me
4. Sally; I
5. Carlos; me
6. Sally; I
7. Sally; me
8. Sally; I
9. Sally; me
10. Sally; I

Lesson 35, Adjectives (P. 47)

Top:
1. bright
2. noisy
3. great
4. clean
5. Three
6. One; funny
7. strange
8. great

Bottom:
Discuss your answers with your instructor.

Lesson 36, Comparing with Adjectives (P. 48)

Top:
1. strangest
2. cooler
3. hottest
4. rainier
5. drier
6. greater

Bottom:
1. biggest
2. harder
3. closer
4. greater
5. calmer or calmest
6. longer

Lesson 37, Using *A* or *An* (P. 49)

Top:

1. a		11. an	
2. an		12. a	
3. a		13. a	
4. a		14. an	
5. an		15. a	
6. a		16. an	
7. a		17. a	
8. a		18. an	
9. a		19. an	
10. a		20. an	

Bottom:
A police officer came to the scene of an accident. An automobile had hit a truck. But it was not an emergency. Neither driver had an injury. The police officer filed a report.

Lesson 38, Adverbs (P. 50)

Top:

HOW?	WHEN?	WHERE?
carefully	later	everywhere
quickly	early	far
happily	now	here
quietly	then	out

Bottom:
1. early — when
2. quietly — how
3. later — when
4. there — where

Lesson 39, Using *Good* and *Well* (P. 51)

Top:
1. good
2. well
3. good
4. well
5. good
6. good
7. well

Bottom:
Bejamin did not have a good time when he was ill. But the doctor did his job well. Soon Benjamin was well enough to return to work. He said it was good to be back. All the other workers were glad Benjamin was well. They really missed his good sense of humor. He has always told jokes very well. He is a good friend to everyone.

Review (P. 52)

The words in bold should be circled.
1. The <u>garden</u> will be full of **flowers**.
2. The <u>family</u> will mow the <u>yard</u>.
3. The **roses** are in the <u>sun</u>.
4. The **birds** love the <u>birdbath</u>.

1. **Greg** bought <u>seeds</u> at **Plant World**.
2. **Greg** scattered the <u>seeds</u>.
3. He waters his <u>plants</u> every **Monday**.
4. He'll have <u>corn</u> in **July**.

1. The daisies <u>grow</u> quickly.   present
2. The roses **were** droopy.   past
3. The pansies **are** colorful.   present

1. rests
2. am
3. was
4. see
5. does
6. go

1. has
2. has
3. have

Review (P. 53)

1. She
2. her
3. I
4. our
5. My
6. them

1. darkest
2. shorter
3. lowest
4. older
5. cleaner
6. greatest

1. quickly
2. softly
3. soon
4. brightly
5. quietly
6. very

1. well
2. well
3. good
4. good
5. well
6. good

Using What You've Learned (P. 54)

Scott is driving to work by himself. He left earlier than usual to get ready for a big meeting. He is making good time. Then suddenly the cars are moving slower than before. Scott needs to be at work on time. He has many things to do before his meeting. The meeting is at eight o'clock. Now all the cars have stopped. Scott looks all around, but he does not see a problem. Finally, the cars start moving again. Scott thinks this is the silliest thing he has ever seen. What was the cause of this traffic jam? Scott has no idea!

Using What You've Learned (P. 55)

Discuss your answer with your instructor.

Lesson 40, Capitalizing Days, Holidays, and Months (P. 56)

Top:
1. Mother's Day
2. winter
3. July
4. Saturday
5. June
6. spring
7. Thursday
8. April

Bottom:
1. This winter I am going to a parade on New Year's Day.
2. The parade is in January.
3. It is on Saturday.
4. Last summer I went to a parade on Labor Day.

Lesson 41, Capitalizing Names of People and Places (P. 57)

Top:
1. Uncle Brian
2. New York
3. Jamie Smith
4. my father
5. Dallas
6. Florida
7. Aunt Sue
8. Charles
9. France
10. Montreal

Bottom:
1. Our theater group put on a play about Nelson Mandela.
2. Did your uncle from San Diego see it?
3. I think Aunt Sarah liked it.
4. Susan Allen had the part of Winnie Mandela.

Lesson 42, Beginning Sentences (P. 58)

1. Have you ever had a family reunion?
2. No, but it sounds like fun.
3. We are having our reunion in Lincoln, Nebraska.
4. Elena is sending out the invitations next week.
5. She hopes that more than 200 people will attend.
6. Our family lives all across North America.
7. It will be exciting to meet some relatives we don't know.
8. Will it be difficult to find everyone?
9. I am not sure.

Lesson 43, Ending Sentences (P. 59)

Top:
1. Guppies can live in a large bowl of water.
2. Does the water need to be cleaned?
3. Look at their pretty colors!
4. How many are there?
5. What a big tail that guppy has!

Bottom:
1. Do you feed guppies dry food?
2. I can't believe how well they swim!
3. The biggest guppy is named Butch.
4. What is the little one's name?
5. I like him the best.

Lesson 44, Abbreviating Names of People and Places (P. 60)

Top:
1. Arthur C. Clarke
2. Mrs. Tolan
3. Cherry Tree Rd.
4. Dr. Spock
5. A. A. Milne
6. Ms. T. Lowry
7. Quimby St.
8. Mr. Stephen King
9. E. M. Thomas

Bottom:
The words in bold should be circled.
mr Tom Sawyer is in a book by **m** Twain.
1. Mr.
2. M.

Lesson 45, Abbreviating Names of Days and Months (P. 61)

Top:
1. Thurs.
2. Aug.
3. Sun.
4. Mar.
5. Tues.
6. Feb.
7. Mon.
8. Sept.
9. Oct.
10. Sat.
11. Dec.
12. Wed.
13. Nov.
14. Fri.
15. Jan.
16. Apr.

Bottom:
The words in bold should be circled.
1. That bill must be paid by **Sat.**, **Sept.** 4th.
2. I have a doctor's appointment on **Fri.**, **Oct.** 31st.

Lesson 46, Using Commas in Sentences (P. 62)

1. Yes, the band was in the parade.
2. Patty, Carlos, and Jo rode on a float.
3. We saw the floats, clowns, and marching bands.
4. The horses, fire engines, and flags came next.

5. No, I didn't stay until the end.
6. Yes, I wanted to stay.
7. We bought juice, nuts, and fruit to eat.
8. Yes, I had a good time.
9. Patty, Carlos, Jo, and I rode home together.

Lesson 47, Writing Letters Correctly (P. 63)

Top:
The words in bold should be circled.
1. New York, New York 10011
2. April 3, 2006
3. **dear gina,**
4. **your** friend,

Bottom:
1. May 7, 2006
2. Miami, Florida 33137
3. Dear Alicia,
4. With love,

Lesson 48, Using Apostrophes to Show Ownership (P. 64)

Top:
1. the pilot's hat
2. the woman's car
3. five dogs' bones
4. a kitten's toys
5. a golfer's hat
6. many men's hats
7. the women's cars
8. a worker's contract
9. ten violins' strings
10. the birds' nests

Bottom:
Discuss your answer with your instructor.

Lesson 49, Using Apostrophes in Contractions (P. 65)

Top:
1. she's
2. we're
3. you'll
4. I've
5. he'd
6. she's

Middle:
1. hasn't
2. isn't
3. weren't
4. I'll
5. that's
6. wouldn't
7. they'll
8. there's

Bottom:
1. Jay hasn't seen that movie.
2. It's about a strange land.
3. One year winter doesn't come.
4. The people don't mind.

Lesson 50, Using Quotation Marks (P. 66)

1. "I need to complete our tax return," said Carl. **or**
   Carl said, "I need to complete our tax return."
2. "I will help you," said Jane. **or**
   Jane said, "I will help you."
3. "Let's use the calculator to total these receipts," said Jane. **or**
   Jane said, "Let's use the calculator to total these receipts."
4. "I hope we get a refund this year," said Carl. **or**
   Carl said, "I hope we get a refund this year."

Review (P. 67)

Top:
The letters in bold should be circled.
1. **mr.** and **mrs. k**amp lived in a house on **may s**treet.
2. **o**ne **s**aturday the couple cleaned the attic.
3. **e**llen found an old letter from **dr. r. m. w**ilson.
4. **t**he letter came all the way from **j**apan!
5. **p**eter found a picture of roses, daisies, and tulips.
6. **d**id **a**unt **j**ulia take that photo on **v**alentine's **d**ay?
7. **n**o, **u**ncle **g**eorge took the photo last **a**pril.
8. **w**hat a mess the attic is!
9. **y**es, **e**llen will clean out the attic next spring.

Bottom:
1. Tues.
2. Fri.
3. Mrs.
4. Elm St.
5. Dec.
6. M. C. Lee
7. Apr.
8. J. R. Adams
9. Feb.
10. Mon.
11. Smith Rd.
12. Mr.
13. Sat.
14. Dr. A. Roberts
15. Ms. N. Lincoln
16. Aug.

Review (P. 68)

Top:

The letters in bold should be circled.

1. **b**irmingham, **a**labama 35205
2. **a**ugust 18, 2006
3. **d**ear **k**im,
4. **y**ours truly
5. **d**ear **m**om,
6. **a**ustin, **t**exas 78753
7. **s**incerely,
8. **d**ear **d**r. **w**est,
9. **y**our friend,
10. **d**ec. 1, 2006

Bottom:

1. "This is Ellen's recipe," said Louisa.
2. Louisa said, "It's her children's favorite."
3. "I'd like to try to make that recipe," said Mike.
4. Mike takes out the chicken, cheese, noodles, and spices.
5. "This recipe doesn't look hard to make," Mike said.
6. "Let's read the recipe together," said Louisa.
7. She asked, "Are the directions printed on the back of the card?"
8. Mike said, "Yes, they're on the back."
9. He said, "I'll grate the cheese first."
10. Mike's apron is untied, so Louisa reties it.
11. Mike doesn't know where the large baking dish is.
12. Louisa says she'll help him look in a minute.

Using What You've Learned (P. 69)

The underlined letters should be circled.

A Hidden Surprise

<u>M</u>s. Anderson's cat is named <u>S</u>am. <u>W</u>hat a big, smart, beautiful cat he is! <u>O</u>ne summer day, <u>M</u>s. Anderson couldn't find him. <u>D</u>o you know where he was? <u>H</u>e was under the porch with three new kittens. <u>M</u>s. Anderson said, "<u>Y</u>our name is <u>S</u>amantha now."

Using What You've Learned (P. 70)

Discuss your answer with your instructor.

 Unit 5 Composition

Lesson 51, Writing Sentences (P. 71)

Discuss your answers with your instructor.

Lesson 52, Writing Paragraphs (P. 72)

Discuss your answers with your instructor.

Lesson 53, Writing Topic Sentences (P. 73)

The following sentences should be underlined:

It is important to plan ahead when you are preparing a dinner for friends.

Set the table before your guests arrive.

Cooking a variety of recipes can help you learn about different cultures.

Lesson 54, Writing Details (P. 74)

The sentence in bold should be circled.

You can make punch look more festive for a party. My friend is a chef in a restaurant. <u>One way is to put whole cloves in the center of orange, lemon, or lime slices.</u> Some people prefer to drink soda at a party. <u>Then float the fruit slices on top of the punch. Or you may wish to add a fruit-filled ice ring or fruit-filled ice cubes to the punch.</u> Buying generic brands saves you money.

Lesson 55, Arranging Details in Order (P. 75)

<u>1</u> It is easy to make tomato cups for salads, such as chicken or tuna. <u>5</u> Then cover and chill the tomatoes. <u>3</u> Next, use a sharp knife to cut each tomato into sections, without cutting all the way through it. <u>4</u> After cutting the tomatoes, spread the sections slightly, and sprinkle a little salt inside. <u>6</u> Finally, place spoonfuls of the salad mixture in the middle of each tomato. <u>2</u> First, place fresh, ripe tomatoes on a cutting board so that the stems are face down.

Lesson 56, Writing with Purpose (P. 76)

Discuss your answers with your instructor.

Lesson 57, Choosing a Topic (P. 77)

Top:
Discuss your answers with your instructor.
Bottom:
Discuss your answers with your instructor.

Lesson 58, How-to Paragraph (P. 78)

Top:
It is easy to make chocolate banana pops.
Bottom:
Discuss your answers with your instructor.

Lesson 59, Writing a How-to Paragraph (P. 79)

Discuss your answers with your instructor.

Lesson 60, Writing an Invitation (P. 80)

Discuss your answer with your instructor.

Lesson 61, Writing a Telephone Message (P. 81)

Discuss your answer with your instructor.

Review (P. 82)

Top:
Discuss your answers with your instructor.

Middle:
The sentence in bold should be circled.

A break between acts in a play is needed. <u>It allows time for the crowd to get up and stretch.</u> Stephanie is a very good gardener. <u>It lets the people in the show get ready for the rest of the play. It also gives the audience time to prepare for the next act.</u>

Bottom:
1. 3
   1
   4
   2
2. 3
   4
   1
   2

Review (P. 83)

Top:

Discuss your answers with your instructor.

Bottom:

Discuss your answers with your instructor.

Using What You've Learned (P. 84)

Discuss your answers with your instructor.

Using What You've Learned (P. 85)

Top:

Discuss your answers with your instructor.

Bottom:

Discuss your answers with your instructor.

 Unit 6 **Study Skills**

Lesson 62, Following Directions (P. 86)

1. south
2. Cook Street
3. west
4. Forest Road
5. 6

Lesson 63, Following Written Directions (P. 87)

1. It describes how to prepare for a flood.
2. First, you should remain calm.
3. So you can find out if there are any special instructions for your community.
4. You should use concrete blocks, bricks, or stacks of boards.

Lesson 64, Grouping (P. 88)

Top:
1. mouse
   monkey
   sheep
   bird
2. bread
   egg
   carrot
   apple
   fish
3. blue
   red
   purple
   orange
4. apple
   orange
   banana
   grape
5. pants
   shirt
   jacket
   hat
6. ball
   circle
   penny
   orange
7. bird
   jet
   rocket
8. Peter
   Mike
   Josh
   Tom
9. Karen
   Pam
   Elaine
   Melanie
10. peas
    carrots
    beans
    corn
11. hammer
    saw
    shovel
    rake

Bottom:

Appliances	Vegetables	Buildings
stove	carrot	house
refrigerator	corn	library
toaster	potato	store

Lesson 65, Using a Table of Contents (P. 89)

1. 6
2. Composition
3. 62
4. Sentences
5. 71
6. Review
7. Unit 3
8. 86
9. 12
10. 17
11. 100
12. 109

Lesson 66, Using an Index (P. 90)

1. the inside back cover
2. 1, 11, 15, 17, 101, 112
3. 1, 6, 14, 17, 100, 112
4. 66, 68, 69, 70, 107, 114
5. no
6. 2, 34, 52, 54, 55, 104, 113
7. Multiple meanings
8. Answers should include three of the following: Apostrophes, Commas, Exclamation points, Periods, Question marks, Quotation marks.
9. Writing process
10. 81, 84, 109
11. 4, 93, 94, 111, 115
12. 3, 63, 68, 70, 107, 114

Lesson 67, Alphabetical Order (P. 91)

1. canoe
2. oar
3. paddle

1. giant
2. glass
3. good

1. ranch
2. town
3. week

1. ball
2. beach
3. bounce

1. east
2. paddle
3. soap

1. pole
2. price
3. pump

Lesson 68, Guide Words (P. 92)

Top:

1. add / chase
2. quack / weep
3. quack / weep
4. add / chase
5. quack / weep
6. add / chase
7. quack / weep
8. quack / weep

Bottom:

1. ill
2. arrow
3. dine
4. job
5. iron
6. weight
7. dent
8. ship
9. across
10. wonder
11. heard
12. post

Lesson 69, Dictionary: Definitions (P. 93)

1. carol
2. call
3. calf, carpet
4. carol
5. Discuss your answers with your instructor.
6. Discuss your answers with your instructor.
7. Discuss your answers with your instructor.

Lesson 69, Dictionary: Definitions (P. 94)

1. 1
2. 1
3. 2
4. 2
5. 2
6. 3
7. 1
8. 2
9. 2
10. 1
11. 1
12. 2
13. 1
14. 1
15. 3
16. 2

Lesson 70, Dictionary: Pronunciation (P. 95)

Top:
1. pull
2. pierce
3. about, taken, pencil, lemon, circus

Bottom:
1. chose
2. letter
3. science
4. carton
5. these
6. measure
7. fuel
8. thimble
9. loyal
10. sure

Review (P. 96)

Top:
1. You can easily put a smoke detector in your home.
2. Decide where you want to put the detector.
3. Put a battery into the bracket.
4. By twisting or snapping it into place.
5. You should check your detector at least once a month.

Middle:
1. May March July April
2. fall spring summer winter
3. apples oranges pears

Bottom:
1. clothes
2. meals
3. colors

Review (P. 97)

1. cage
   lake
   seen
2. bat
   bee
   blue

3. plow
   press
   puff
1. 50
2. 1, 59, 67, 69, 70, 102, 112
3. 1, 7, 8, 14, 16, 17, 100, 112

1. to hunt
2. to be on one's feet
3. the stem of a plant
4. to put up with

1. awful
2. rhyme
3. van
4. hour
5. weather

Using What You've Learned (P. 98)
Top:

Fruits	Canned	Vegetables
bananas	canned soup	potatoes
apples		lettuce
		broccoli

Frozen	Meat
frozen orange juice	chicken
	hamburger
	bacon

Bottom:
1. Using What You've Learned
2. 37
3. 92
4. Using a Table of Contents
5. 13
6. Sentences

Using What You've Learned (P. 99)
Top:

Discuss your answers with your instructor.
Bottom:
Discuss your answers with your instructor.

 Final Reviews

Final Review, Unit 1 (P. 100)
1. S
2. A
3. A
4. A
5. A
6. A
7. S
8. A
9. A
10. A

1. to
2. too
3. hear
4. two
5. there
6. here
7. They're

Final Review, Unit 1 (P. 101)
1. 2
2. 1
3. 1
4. 2

1. unable, not able
2. relive, live again
3. repay, pay again
4. untrue, not true

1. worker; someone who works
2. dryer; something that dries
3. visitor; someone who visits
4. marker; something that marks

The words in bold should be circled.
1. someone
2. **he's**
3. **I'll**
4. daylight

Final Review, Unit 2 (P. 102)

1. S
2. Q
3. E
4. C
5. X
6. Q
7. S
8. X
9. S
10. C

The words in bold should be circled.

1. <u>Mr. and Mrs. Fleming</u> **took care of their grandchildren on Saturday**.
2. <u>Mr. Fleming</u> **bought a pizza for lunch**.
3. <u>Mrs. Fleming</u> **played games with the children**.
4. <u>Mr. Fleming</u> **read a book to the children**.
5. <u>The book</u> **was about a knight**.
6. <u>The children</u> **asked if they could watch cartoons**.
7. <u>Mrs. Fleming</u> **turned on some cartoons**.
8. <u>Everyone</u> **laughed at the silly cartoons**.
9. <u>Mr. and Mrs. Fleming</u> **baked cookies for the children**.
10. <u>It</u> **was time for the children to go home**.

Final Review, Unit 2 (P. 103)

1. Dan car-pooled and worked with Alex.
2. Vicenté and Tammy wanted to apply for a new job.
3. They worked today, but they were off last Monday.

4. Vicenté works inside the plant, and Tammy works outside the plant.
5. You can apply for the new job, or you can continue working at your current job.

1. Mark enjoys all kinds of sports. His favorite sport is soccer.
2. Mark's wife used to play soccer. She was on a team in high school.
3. Mark finds a photo of his wife playing soccer. He shows it to his friend Jamal.
4. Jamal's wife is in the photo. His wife used to play soccer, too.

Final Review, Unit 3 (P. 104)

1. P inch
2. S toes
3. S buses
4. P box
5. S carts
6. P wrench

1. C Discuss your answer with your instructor.
2. P state
3. C Discuss your answer with your instructor.
4. P lake

The word in bold should be circled.

1. Kate <u>lives</u> in Chicago. present
2. I <u>visited</u> her in June. past
3. Diane **was** in Chicago last year. past

1. saw
2. buy
3. runs
4. have
5. was
6. did

Final Review, Unit 3 (P. 105)

1. him
2. it
3. His
4. they
5. his
6. he
7. they
8. his
9. I
10. us

---

1. Dinosaurs were once the <u>largest</u> reptiles on Earth.
2. <u>Some</u> dinosaurs ate <u>green</u> plants.
3. <u>Other</u> animals felt <u>safe</u> around dinosaurs that ate plants.
4. <u>Some</u> dinosaurs ate <u>fresh</u> meat.
5. It was <u>dangerous</u> for <u>other</u> animals to be <u>close</u> to one of <u>these</u> <u>hungry</u> dinosaurs.

---

1. Many kinds of dinosaurs lived <u>together</u>.
2. Scientists have <u>carefully</u> studied how dinosaurs lived.
3. There are no dinosaurs alive <u>today</u>.
4. Scientists do not know <u>exactly</u> what happened to them, since it was <u>so</u> long <u>ago</u>.
5. They have worked <u>very</u> hard to find reasons why the dinosaurs died.

Final Review, Unit 4 (P. 106)

1. December
2. winter
3. Monday
4. my daughter
5. Louise
6. New Year's Day
7. California
8. Denver
9. Thanksgiving
10. Canada
11. Tomás
12. store

The letters in bold should be circled.

1. **m**y family and I live in **o**rlando, **f**lorida.
2. **w**e moved here from **h**untsville, **t**exas, last summer.
3. **i** work in a museum.
4. **i**t is called the **c**harles **c**. **a**dler **m**useum.
5. **t**he museum is north of my home.
6. **i**t is on **j**ones **s**treet near **a**cademy **t**heater.
7. **t**he museum is closed on **s**undays and **m**ondays.
8. **m**s. **n**. **k**elly is my boss.
9. **m**s. **k**elly is getting the museum ready for a large dinosaur display.
10. **t**he display will be set up on the first **t**uesday in **m**arch.
11. **i**'m going to help make sure the display is perfect.
12. **s**tudents from **o**ak **s**prings **e**lementary will be the first to view our dinosaurs.

Final Review, Unit 4 (P. 107)

1. Ms. N. Kelly asked, "Are you ready to set up the dinosaur display?"
2. Yes, I was ready for the dinosaurs to arrive.
3. The workers brought in dinosaur bones, footprints, and models.
4. I didn't count all the boxes, but I could tell that this dinosaur display was going to be huge.
5. One worker said, "I can't get this model through the door."
6. "You'll have to take it in through the back," I said.
7. I worked on Wednesday, Thursday, and Friday setting up the display.
8. I asked my boss if she liked the display.
9. Ms. Kelly said, "Yes, I am very pleased with the job you have done."
10. "I'd bet the children can't wait to see the dinosaurs," I said.

1. Dear Zach,
2. June 1, 2006
3. Houston, Texas 77072
4. Sincerely,
5. April 9, 2006
6. Your friend,
7. Dear Jesse,
8. Kansas City, Missouri 64114

Final Review, Unit 5 (P. 108)

1. Discuss your answer with your instructor.
2. Discuss your answer with your instructor.
3. Discuss your answer with your instructor.

The sentences in bold should be circled.

<u>3</u> Next, practice saying your speech in front of a mirror. <u>2</u> The first thing you can do to make yourself feel better is to get used to being on a stage. <u>4</u> Finally, ask some friends or family members if they will listen to you practice. <u>1</u> **Most people get scared when they have to give a speech.**

<u>2</u> First, she pulled all of the weeds in her garden. <u>1</u> **Yesterday Ms. Yamata worked in her garden.** <u>4</u> When Ms. Yamata was finished, she drank a large glass of lemonade. <u>3</u> Then she planted some tulips, daisies, and roses.

Final Review, Unit 5 (P. 109)

Discuss your answer with your instructor.

(Date) Today's Date
(Time) Time
(To) Tony
(Message) Possible answer: Call Kim at work about a computer problem. The number is 555-9487.
(From) Claudia

Final Review, Unit 6 (P. 110)

1. east
2. Oak Road
3. Town Hall

Breakfast	Dinner	Snacks
toast	fish	popcorn
pancakes	spaghetti	raisins

1. in the front of the book
2. titles of parts of the book and page numbers on which the parts can be found
3. the back of the book
4. in alphabetical order

Final Review, Unit 6 (P. 111)

1. rake
   sat
   scare
2. cause
   cheer
   teeth

leather / lie

1. 1
2. 2

1. noisy
2. drawing
3. summer
4. fuss
5. aware
6. honor

Check What You've Learned (P. 112)

A. 1. H
   2. S
   3. H
   4. A

B. 1. 2
   2. 3

C. 1. P
   2. C
   3. S
   4. C

D. 1. I am
   2. she will
   3. he is or he has
   4. can not

The words in bold should be circled.

E. 1. Q **Where are** <u>you</u> **going**?
   2. S <u>I</u> **am going to Mexico**.
   3. C <u>(You)</u> **Pack plenty of sunscreen**.
   4. E <u>I</u> **can't wait until next week**!

Check What You've Learned (P. 113)

F. 1. Jane and Andy had an appointment.
   2. Jessie lives in north Glenview, and he works in south Glenview.

G. 1. I went to an interview. I hope I get the job.
   2. Candace has a date. She's going to a movie.

The words in bold should be circled.

H. 1. S **book**
   2. P <u>Fridays</u>
   3. P **chairs**
   4. S <u>California</u>

I. 1. L
   2. H
   3. A

J. 1. present
   2. past

Check What You've Learned (P. 114)

K. 1. my
   2. They
   3. them

L. 1. adverb
   2. adjective

M.   8406 <u>C</u>anton <u>R</u>d<u>.</u>
          <u>R</u>awlins<u>,</u> <u>W</u>yoming 82301
          <u>A</u>pr<u>.</u> 12<u>,</u> 1994

Dear <u>M</u>s<u>.</u> <u>B</u>urke<u>,</u>
  <u>I</u>'ve been living in your apartment complex for three years<u>.</u> <u>S</u>ome people ask<u>,</u> <u>"D</u>oesn't <u>M</u>s<u>.</u> <u>B</u>urke care about her apartments<u>?"</u> <u>Y</u>es<u>,</u> <u>I</u> think you do<u>.</u> <u>I</u> say, <u>"I</u> think <u>M</u>s<u>.</u> <u>B</u>urke's apartments are great<u>."</u> <u>M</u>aybe you could fix the plumbing<u>,</u> wallpaper<u>,</u> and carpeting<u>.</u> <u>T</u>hen people would be happier<u>.</u>
                    <u>S</u>incerely<u>,</u>
                    <u>P</u>at <u>J</u>anson

N. Discuss your answers with your instructor.

Check What You've Learned (P. 115)

O. 1. 3

2. 2

3. 1

P. 1. handle

2. honest

3. hope

4. hour

Q. 1. pass, peace

2. place

3. peace